BEHIND THE WIRE

FOR MAY

BEHIND THE WIRE

ALLIED PRISONERS OF WAR IN HITLER'S GERMANY

PHILIP KAPLAN & JACK CURRIE

Pen & Sword
AVIATION

First published in Great Britain in 2012 by
PEN & SWORD AVIATION
An imprint of
Pen & Sword Books Ltd
47 Church Street
Barnsley
South Yorkshire
S70 2AS

ISBN 978 1 78159 044 7

A CIP catalogue record for this book is
available from the British Library

Printed and bound in England
By CPI Group (UK) Ltd, Croydon, CR0 4YY

Pen & Sword Books Ltd incorporates the Imprints of Pen & Sword Aviation,
Pen & Sword Family History, Pen & Sword Maritime, Pen & Sword Military,
Pen & Sword Discovery, Pen & Sword Politics, Pen & Sword Atlas,
Pen & Sword Archaeology, Wharncliffe Local History, Wharncliffe True Crime,
Wharncliffe Transport, Pen & Sword Select, Pen & Sword Military Classics,
Leo Cooper, The Praetorian Press, Claymore Press, Remember When,
Seaforth Publishing and Frontline Publishing

For a complete list of Pen & Sword titles please contact
PEN & SWORD BOOKS LIMITED
47 Church Street, Barnsley, South Yorkshire, S70 2AS, England
E-mail: enquiries@pen-and-sword.co.uk
Website: www.pen-and-sword.co.uk

CONTENTS

ACKNOWLEDGEMENTS

The authors are grateful to the following people for their kind assistance and contributions in the development of this book: Don Ackerson, Roger Armstrong, George Behling, Quentin Bland, Bob Braham, May Butcher, Douglas Connolly, Luther Cox, Aidan Crawley, Albert Clark, Kate Currie, Bob Doherty, James Doolittle, Han Geurts, Bill Harvey, Larry Hewin, John Hurd, Charles Johnson, Burton Joseph, Claire Kaplan, Joseph Kaplan, Neal Kaplan, Frank Kautzmann, Walter Konantz, Eric Lapham, Robert Long, Frank Madrid, Barry Mahon, Walker Mahurin, Eric Marsden, Margaret Mayhew, William McCarran, Bob Neary, Merle Olmsted, Geoffrey Page, Duane Reed, Kenneth Simmons, Dale Smith, Bobby Stark, Peter Townsend, John Vietor, Don Walsh, Chuck Yeager, Hubert Zemke.

Particular thanks to author / historian Arthur A. Durand for the kind, generous permission to quote from *Stalag Luft III*, his superb and "masterly recreation of virtually every aspect of the daily prison experience and a testament to the prisoners' ingenuity, perseverance, and raw courage against monumental odds."

INTRODUCTION

The vilest deeds like poison weeds
Bloom well in prison air:
It is only what is good in Man
That wastes and withers there:
Pale anguish keeps the heavy gate,
And the warder is Despair.
　　　—Oscar Wilde

We were not heroes . . . but we did our best, in unique circumstances, to continue the war and to come home with honor.
　　　—General Albert P. Clark

Most of the many American and British airmen who were brought down in European skies during World War II to become prisoners of the Germans fell into three distinct categories. The first were those who thought only of escape. They dedicated themselves to getting over, or under, the wire to freedom and rejoining their units in England, Italy, or North Africa. They spent nearly all of their time plotting, planning, and preparing for their own escape attempts and for those of their fellow prisoners. The idea of breaking out sustained and motivated them for the duration of their captivity.

Another group of prisoners had an entirely different attitude about their situation. Shrouded in bitterness at their fate, they retreated into depression, turned inward and took little part in any camp activities. They lay in their bunks and read or faced the wall, brooding about the injustice of their circumstance. They achieved little during their captivity and contributed even less to the well being of their comrades. Many suffered excessively and needlessly for their self-imposed isolation.

Finally, there were those who were quick to make the mental adjustment, who resolved to understand and come to terms with their new circumstance in the best, most productive and worthwhile ways they could. They soon evaluated the situation and, while struggling with the same everyday problems as their fellow kriegies, the German nickname for Allied prisoners of war, they simply got on with it. They repaired sanitation facilities, washhouses and latrines; improvised to supplement their limited cooking capacity, and worked to significantly improve the camp medical services. They built recreational sites, theaters and other camp facilities. They reasoned that they were stuck in a situation for the duration of the war and they set out to make something of their lot, to find opportunities and exploit them to the fullest. They were high achievers, many of them leaders and people of considerable skill and talent who used their gifts to advance their cause and that of their fellows. Their motivation, determination and guts got them through the captivity. Many matured greatly and actually gained something from the experience.

All prisons are brimming over with innocence.
It is those who cram their fellows into them,
in the name of empty ideas,
who are the only guilty ones.
—Jean Anouilh

PROLOGUE

THE AIR over Debden, England, the home base of the 4th Fighter Group, Eighth US Army Air Force, on the afternoon of 13th April 1944 was full of excitement. The Fourth's leading ace, Captain Don Gentile, celebrated the completion of his tour of duty by 'beating up' the airfield in a low pass that was to be the last flying moment for his legendary P-51 Mustang, *Shangri-La*. The plane struck the ground and, with its airframe broken, became a write-off. Captain Gentile was unhurt in the incident. A few hundred miles away at about the same time, in the skies over Belgium, another Eighth Air Force airplane, a B-17 Flying Fortress called *The Royal Flush*, of the 384th Bomb Group (H) which was based at Grafton Underwood in Northamptonshire, was also falling out of the sky.

Twenty-one-year-old Charles W. Johnson of Louisville, Kentucky, was the right waist gunner on *The Royal Flush* that spring day. He remembered his experience like this:

"Our target that day was the ball-bearing works at Schweinfurt. Shortly before reaching the target, we were hit head-on by a swarm of ME 109s. Six of our (384BG) B-17s were shot down. We regrouped and hit our target. Two more B-17s that were badly shot up had to crash-land in France on their return trip. The remaining 13 bombers of our group were about 12 minutes from the Channel when I saw the first two bursts of flak heading our way. One of them got us between the number two engine and the cockpit. According to Dewayne Bennett, a friend of mine who was aboard a B-17 off to our left in the formation, our left wing folded over the fuselage and then the plane exploded into a huge fireball. He had no choice but to fly through the junk of our plane. He thought it a miracle that they made it through unscathed.

"When we got hit I was thrown down on the floor and pinned there. I managed to roll on my side and clamp one buckle of my chute to my harness. I was passing out. My last thought was: This is a hell of a way to die. I remember that the plane seemed to sort of shudder, which I later assumed was the explosion. When I came to, my body was in a reclining position and everything was so quiet and peaceful. I realized I was falling and pulled my rip-cord. I immediately thought about my other snap, but everything held.

When the chute opened I had a sharp pain in my right leg and when I looked down to see if I still had a right leg, I saw the ground meeting me.

"I don't remember hitting, so I was awake maybe only three or four seconds, just long enough to open my chute. I have no idea how long I lay there before I awoke. When I did, I was slumped over in a sitting position and my harness and parachute were gone. No doubt they were taken by a member of the Underground. I don't know if they thought I was dead, but I know they could not afford to take anyone who was seriously wounded.

"A little later, an older man approached me and motioned for me to get up and follow him. I saw a twig on the ground, picked it up and snapped it in two and made a sweeping motion with my hand to indicate to him that my lower body was broken. I then said: 'Go before you get killed.'

"I looked around and in the distance a half mile or so away. I saw someone's 'chute in a tree and about half that distance away was an inflated life raft. None of my crew. . . nothing. About a block or so away was a farmhouse with five or six people gathered in front and looking my way. They didn't dare come any closer. A little later I dragged myself toward a small drainage ditch running alongside the little lane that ran to the farmhouse, thinking that if the Germans didn't spot me, maybe the Underground would consider doing something for me.

"Realizing that I had no chance, I decided to unload everything except my escape pictures. I took out my hunting knife and made a three-sided cut in the sod. I laid it back and scooped out a hole and when I was ready, I waved it over my head for the Belgian family to see. It contained a large amount of money, rice paper maps, and various types of compasses. I then buried it and smoothed out the area. I'll wager a Blue Jay would have had a hard time locating it. I then took my knife and scabbard and threw it as far as possible into some tall grass on the other side of the lane. Then I lay down in the small depression of the ditch and waited.

"By this time the shock started to wear off. About the only thing that didn't hurt was my hair. I wondered where the rest of my crew were. I could see the 'chute in the tree, but no one was strapped to it. I felt truly lost and lonesome. Did they get away? Were they all killed? Am I just imagining all this? I spent many a sleepless night after that—just wondering. It wasn't until about eight months later, when I received my first letter from my mother, that I found out what had happened to some of them. I learned then that three othersof my crew had survived and had evaded the enemy and were taken in by the Belgian Underground.

"I waited an hour or so and then heard a shout.
I saw that I was surrounded by rifle-toting German soldiers. More shouts. I didn't do a thing, and then they fired. Bullets hit the dirt around me and came in a little closer. More shouts. Still I didn't do anything. More bullets. It finally dawned on me to hold up my arms. The Sergeant came up and put his pistol between my eyes and searched me.

"Two of the soldiers then went to a nearby barn and returned with a homemade ladder which they used as a stretcher. They placed me on it and took me to an automobile and laid me in the back seat.
I was taken to a first aid station or doctor's office and a nurse cut my clothes off, cleaned my two wounds and placed a splint on my leg. She then started to wash my face, but stopped. She picked up a mirror, the type with a long handle, and put it in front of my face. Jesus Christ! I was covered with blood. Some of the blood, no doubt, was mine, but I think most of it was someone elses. I was then put on a real stretcher, covered with a blanket and taken out to another car, a 1937 Oldsmobile.

Half of the town was looking on. Mostly young girls and older people. To get me in, they removed the blanket, which left me totally naked from the waist down. I know my face turned bright red, but it didn't phase the young girls.

"On the way to Brussels, the auto travelled at a leisurely pace except when we approached a town. The siren would start and we would pick up speed until we got through. Other than me, there was the driver, a soldier sitting next to him, and a soldier on each side standing on the running boards. All three had machine-pistols.

"When we arrived in Brussels there was some traffic and we were travelling behind a car with a lot of people who were standing on the rear end and when they saw me they gave the V for victory sign.

"I was taken to a hospital where I was given a bed in an annex that held only P.O.W.s. Several days later, after the swelling had gone down in my leg, they put a cast on it. They put only iodine or something on my wounds.

"The first morning I was there, a "Red Cross" woman interrogated me. I gave her my name, rank and serial number. She wanted to know our target, the types of bombs we used, my group number and the whole ball of wax. She got nothing. I got put in an isolation room. I was brought back to the ward that night. The next morning she went through the same routine. Same results. This went on until 16th April. On the morning of the 17th, an orderly came to my bed and I thought, 'not again.' He looked at my identification slate, looked at me, looked again at my slate. Then, the rascal sang 'Happy Birthday' to me. He made my day. So you see . . . they weren't all that bad.

"That "Red Cross" person was about as much Red Cross as I was a non-combatant.

"Within a few days, a dozen or so of us P.O.W.s left Brussels. We were on a train going down the valley. It was beautiful. Castles on the hilltops. Picturesque villages and homes, and anti-aircraft batteries everywhere. We finally came to a large city and changed trains. While waiting for our train, we were put on 'display' in front of the station. Things weren't going too badly until a wounded SS trooper showed up. He had one arm missing. He got the crowd all worked up until I thought we had had it. One old woman came up to me with fists flying, stopped and cleared her throat and spat the whole gob in my face. I almost struck her, but caught myself in time, because that was all they needed to finish us. Then she also called me a 'Verdamt Americanishe Flieger Gangster.'

"We finally arrived at Dulag Luft. I was there only overnight, and was sent to a nearby hospital. After a week or so in the cast, they removed it and I was given a cane. They could at least have given me a crutch. I had to use the cane as a sort of pogo stick.

"I was sent to another hospital where I stayed only for a day or two before being sent on to a P.O.W. hospital. It was run by a combination of Wehrmacht and Luftwaffe officers. There were several British medical personnel there who had been captured in Africa. I kept having constant upper back, shoulder and neck spasms, and my knee was not mending properly. Also, my memory at times was a complete blank. The cast on my right leg was changed perhaps five or six times, from my hip to my ankle bone.

"I left the hospital on the 5th November 1944. On the way to

Stalag Luft IV, we were parked overnight in a rail yard in Berlin. The air raid alarms sounded, searchlights lit up the sky and anti-aircraft batteries went into action. The RAF was attacking. "That "Red Cross" person was about as much real Red Cross as I was a non-combatant.

"Within a few days, a dozen or so of us P.O.W.s left Brussels. We were on a train going down the valley. It was beautiful. Castles on the hilltops. Picturesque villages and homes, and anti-aircraft batteries everywhere. We finally came to a large city and changed trains. While waiting for our train, we were put on 'display' in front of the station. Things weren't going too badly until a wounded SS trooper showed up. He had one arm missing. He got the crowd all worked up until I thought we had had it. One old woman came up to me with fists flying, stopped and cleared her throat and spat the whole gob in my face. I almost struck her, but caught myself in time, because that was all they needed to finish us. Then she also called me a 'Verdamt Americanishe Flieger Gangster.'

"We finally arrived at Dulag Luft. I was there only overnight, and was sent to a nearby hospital. After a week or so in the cast, they removed it and I was given a cane. They could at least have given me a crutch. I had to use the cane as a sort of pogo stick.

"I was sent to another hospital where I stayed only for a day or two before being sent on to a P.O.W. hospital. It was run by a combination of Wehrmacht and Luftwaffe officers. There were several British medical personnel there who had been captured in Africa. I kept having constant upper back, shoulder and neck spasms, and my knee was not mending properly. Also, my memory at times was a complete blank. The cast on my right leg was changed perhaps five or six times, from my hip to my ankle bone.

"I left the hospital on the 5th November 1944. On the way to Stalag Luft IV, we were parked overnight in a rail yard in Berlin. The air raid alarms sounded, searchlights lit up the sky and anti-aircraft batteries went into action. The RAF was attacking. Our guards than just water. Some of us would go to the compound dump and root out old dry hard bread. If you scraped off the dirt etc. you could re-wet it, then squeeze out the excess water and eat it. I would scavenge the old discarded prune seeds, crack them open and eat the kernels. Bitter, but food. That potato bread was something else. As long as it wasn't sliced, it wasn't bad, but slice it or cut and you had better eat it, because it would quickly get as hard as a brick. And whatever you do, don't drop a loaf on your foot.

"Several of our top fighter pilots were in our camp. Colonel Hubert 'Hub' Zemke was the ranking officer and Col. Francis Gabreski was in our compound. When things were nearing the end, Col. Zemke was told by the Kommandant that he had orders to evacuate the camp to Lubeck. Col. Zemke asked him what would happen if we refused to go? He was told that there had been enough bloodshed already. Of course, we were fully responsible for whatever happened.

"The next day they started demolishing the Flak school next to our camp. We could also hear them blowing up the installations at the nearby airfield. That night they machine-gunned and blew up the guard towers at the camp.

"The next morning someone went to headquarters and turned on the BBC and the P.A. system in the compounds. The BBC was broadcasting the 'Hit Parade,' and the song they were playing was Don't Fence Me In."

From the Geneva Convention relative to the treatment of prisoners of war: Except as otherwise hereinafter indicated, every person captured or interned by a belligerent power because of the war is, during the period of such captivity or internment, a prisoner of war, and is entitled to be recognized and treated as such under the laws of war.

DOWNED

AT 0130 AM ON 22nd June 1943, a Wellington bomber of No. 429 Squadron, RCAF, flying in bright moonlight, 20,000 feet above the frontier between Belgium and the Netherlands, was hit by flak and set on fire. The wireless operator baled out safely; the other four crew members were blown out of the aircraft when it exploded. Of these, only the pilot and the navigator, Flying Officer Eric Lapham, both RAF men, had sufficient altitude to deploy their parachutes before they hit the ground. After two days on the run, with the help and guidance of a Belgian couple and a Dutchman, they reached a small town in Flanders, from where they intended to board a train to France. They were stopped, however, by two gendarmes at a road block and, after a night in a police cell, they were handed over to the Germans and questioned. Where had they come from, and who had aided them? Where had they acquired the civilian clothes, and the bicycles? Their explanations, that they had broken into a house to steal the clothes and found the cycles unattended, were greeted with derision. If they could not offer a better story than that, they could be treated as spies, and they must surely know what that meant.

It was the classic problem of the captured evader: how to establish your credentials without betraying the very people who had helped you. Lapham and his pilot stuck doggedly to their story, and tried to give no sign of recognition when, clearly with deliberate intent, they were allowed to glimpse two of their helpers, both in German hands.

The airmen had been warned, back at base, about an enemy technique of planting English-speaking Germans in RAF uniform among captured RAF men to elicit information. When two apparently British fliers joined them in their cell, the initial exchanges were heavy with suspicion until it transpired that all four men had been born and raised in Bristol. "It was remarkable," wrote Eric Lapham, "how one's morale was strengthened by the knowledge that, whatever happened, one of your own kind could vouch for the fact that you survived your crash and were seen alive and well."

The outcome, for Lapham and his pilot, was to be long months behind the wire of prisoner-of-war camps; for the brave Belgian housewife, two years in concentration camps; for the young Dutchman, Johan Vierbergenweg, a German firing squad.

"The Bloody 100th" Bomb Group of the 8th US Air Force led an attack on Braunschweig on 15th March 1944. The lead navigator, 1st Lieutenant Burton M. Joseph, was flying his 25th mission, which was to be—in both senses—the last one of his tour. Turning onto the bomb run from the IP (initial point) his B-17, My Achin' Back, was hit in the forward fuselage by an 88 mm flak shell, and fire broke out immediately. Burt Joseph suffered flash burns to the face and flak wounds in his hands. Both the first and second pilots and five members of the crew perished with the stricken bomber; Joseph, with the top turret gunner and the bombardier, made their escape. Not wanting, as he reported later, "to be the object of further German target practice", he waited until he reached the cover of the cloud undercast before he pulled the ripcord of his parachute. As he emerged into the clear, he saw below him "a vast sea of flame". He landed in the smouldering ruins of a house and received more burns to his head and hands. Nor was that his only problem: "An angry mob of civilians was moving towards me. They would have most certainly torn me apart if a Wehrmacht soldier hadn't gotten to me first. That man held them off with his rifle and undoubtely saved my life."

Some painful hours ensued before Joseph's injuries received any more than cursory attention, and it was only after several days and interrupted journeys to Dulag Luft at Oberursel that he came "to feel the full impact of his new situation: I was a POW in Germany."

On 11th April 1944, a force of more than nine hundred B-17s and B-24s set out to attack aircraft plants in north and east Germany. Among the sixty-four bombers which did not return was Battlin' Betty of the 401st Bomb Group, based at Deenethorpe in Northamptonshire. The aeroplane was piloted by Lieutenant Francis Shaw, and the ball turret gunner was Sergeant John Hurd. It was the crew's eleventh mission. They were heading east in the area of Hannover when their bomber was hit by gunfire, two engines were knocked out, and a piece of shrapnel pierced Hurd's turret. "It hit me in the right butt," he said, "and I can think of worse places." Shaw gave the order to abandon the aircraft, the crew baled out safely, and were taken prisoner as soon as they ouched down.

Hurd's wound was treated, he was interrogated briefly, and the crew were taken east, travelling in a box-car through Frankfurt into Austria. "It was a little uncomfortable," said Hurd, "because I couldn't sit so well". On 17th April, Hurd was imprisoned in Stalag 17B, near the town of Krems, on the river Danube between Linz and Vienna—some 800 miles from his base in England and 6,000 from his home in California.

One of Britain's best known combat fliers was Wing Commander Bob Braham. Between August 1940 and May 1944, he shot down twenty-nine German aircraft, attacked enemy shipping and shot up troop trains. With three DSOs, three DFCs and an AFC, he was Britain's most decorated fighter pilot. Like all the great aces, Braham embodied the offensive spirit, and he was not at all pleased when, in June 1944, he was assigned to the staff of the 2nd Tactical Air Force, with instructions that he could only fly a mission if he obtained the AOC's authority. It was with that permission that he borrowed a Mark 6 Mosquito from No. 21 Squadron on 25th June and, with his Australian navigator Don Walsh, took off from West Raynham in Norfolk for a daylight intruder operation to the German Baltic coast.

Crossing the North Sea at low level, it seems likely that the Mossie was spotted by a German warship, and its course reported to the defences, for it was "bounced" over Denmark by a pair of Fw-190s. In his exciting story "Scramble", Braham blamed himself for this, and for the outcome of the ensuing combat, which ended when he landed on the shore of the Jutland peninsula with his aircraft badly damaged. As he and Walsh ran from the burning plane, the enemy fighters swooped low above them and the leader waved his hand. Burying their maps and Mae Wests, the two men made for cover in the dunes, but were quickly halted by a burst of gunfire from a Luftwaffe patrol. They were taken to the airfield at Esjberg, searched, briefly questioned, and locked in the guardhouse cells.

The next day, on a slow train journey to Dulag Luft near Frankfurt, Braham fully realized the nature of his plight. "The many stops," he wrote, "annoyed our guards who seemed to hold us responsible for all the bomb damage in Germany. Civilians and soldiers shouted abuse at us. We were called 'Luft-gangsters' and threatened with violence. During the night some drunken soldiers tried to enter our compartment . . . one of them drew his bayonet. For the first time in my life my knees were knocking and I had to grab them so that my fright wouldn't be too obvious . . . it seemed that our choice was to sit tight and be lynched by the mob, or to jump through the carriage door and be shot in the back by our guards. Then a young SS soldier in black battledress shouldered his way in and shouted an order. The effect was miraculous. They immediately dispersed. He sat next to us and looked us up and down with disdain as though to say 'Well, Englishmen, you can thank me for saving your worthless hides.' "

How Don Ackerson came to be a 'guest' of the Third Reich is explained by the former bombardier who served with the 547th Squadron, 384th Bomb Group, stationed at Grafton Underwood, England, in April 1944: "Somewhere in the Luxemburg area, we had our first fighter attacks on the lead group. They were about 20 Me-109s who made a pass and then went over to the side and played around for awhile. A few minutes later, we were hit by about 30 FW-190s from 12 and 11 o'clock and almost level. Our ship was hit on that first pass and number three engine caught fire. The burning engine was feathered at once but the fire spread through the wing and into the bomb bay, melting the bulkhead away. The radio operator informed the pilot and he then gave the order to bale out. The navigator then, after making sure that I had heard the order, baled out followed by the engineer. I was behind the engineer as the bombs were still in and I was trying to get them out.

"I left immediately after the bombs were away. I pulled a partially delayed jump, delaying for a few thousand feet, lost consciousness from lack of oxygen or the jerk of the chute opening, and came to at about 18,000 feet and watched our P-51 escort, which was late that day, circle around me. I floated quietly down. It took about 16 minutes. I had a good landing in a plowed field with a farmer shooting at me with a rifle while I was coming down. I could see home guard soldiers running up the road and they took me into custody kicking me because I said 'nein' when they said 'for you the war is over!' They kicked me all the way into a nearby town where we were searched and put in a youth camp guardhouse for a few hours.

"We had three others in the guardhouse, including a gunner with a big piece of flak in his ankle. We couldn't get any medical help for him. That night we were taken in a truck around the country picking up other boys. We spent the rest of the night and most of the next day at an airport also in a guardhouse. We were loosely guarded and could have jumped out the window, but we thought this was what they wanted. Late on the afternoon of the 14th we went by truck to Dulag Luft for interrogation. I got a good scare in Dulag Luft. All of us got a physical and when they saw that I was circumsized, they asked if I was Jewish. For about two days I would have another 'physical' and another interrogation every hour or so. I couldn't seem to make them believe that I was a Methodist whose father was a bit ahead of the times in male hygiene matters. I spent two days in solitary and was sent to the transient camp next door. We stayed there until the morning of the 18th when we left by train for Stalag Luft 1 at Barth. We got there on the 22nd of April 1944 and left on the 13th of May 1945, 13 months to the day after being shot down. I can't remember a thing about the train ride except that we were scared to death of being bombed or shot up by our own planes."

John Vietor was an instructor pilot in B-24 Liberator bombers until December 1943, when he was sent to Lecce, Italy as a Squadron Commander replacement for the 345th Squadron, 98th Bomb Group, 15th US Air Force. He described the day he became a POW in Germany:

"On the morning of Friday, February 25, 1944, the sergeant in charge of headquarters knocked on the door at 4:30. My roommate and I struggled sleepily in the half-light of dawn to put on our heated flying suits, boots, gloves and coveralls. We hurried to our jeep and bounced our way up to 'briefing.'

"The sun was beginning to brighten the lovely Italian landscape as we drove back to the mess, but the sky was still overcast. We stopped on the way to buy eggs for breakfast from a peasant. I had a strange premonitory feeling that these might be the last eggs I would eat for some time.

"After a breakfast of eggs, Spam, canned orange juice, we picked up the rest of our flying equipment and whipped our jeep over the red clay to our ships. Using the entire runway because of gas and bomb load, we took off at precisely eight. At 11:00 a.m. we were at 25,000 feet crossing Austria into Germany.

"Shortly after the command, "Bomb bay doors open," we felt a thump shudder throughout the plane. I thought we'd lost an engine but the readings were okay. An excited voice on the interphone barked Gunner to Pilot. Gunner to Pilot . . . controls shot away by flak! We hopefully flipped on the automatic flight control equipment but it too, was inoperative. Now we were faced with a critical decision. We could salvo our bombs and try to turn back and head for Switzerland, thereby possibly saving the ship and all the crew. On the other hand, we had flown a long way and were only five minutes from the target. It would be a shame to waste those bombs. We might be able to drop them on the target and still turn and make it back to the base with luck. So we continued steadily over the target and dropped our bombs.

"As we turned off the target, on our left we saw swarms of ME-109s coming up to meet us. We were at the mercy of fifty to sixty fighters. No. 1 and No. 4 engines were feathered. After the fighters hit us, the right wing tip and right rudder were gone—and the interphone and oxygen shot away. The order was 'bale out.'

"As soon as the rest of the crew was successfully away, I took over what was left of the controls while Lieutenant Bowman put on his chute; I held her as best I could until she started to spin. I felt a sharp sting in my right leg . . . a .30 calibre bullet. I crawled back towards the bomb bay. I hastily adjusted my chute, taking off my gloves to fasten it more securely. The pressure of the centrifugal force of the spin made it difficult for me to reach the bomb bays and I had a moment of terror and panic, not from the fear of jumping, but from the fear that I might be trapped and unable to pull myself out. Somehow I managed to pull myself clear, almost unconscious from lack of oxygen. It was only by the most tremendous exertion of will power and concentration that I remembered to pull the ripcord . . .

"The rough jerk of the chute shroud lines snapped me into consciousness. It was difficult to breathe in the thin air and, gasping and panting, I struggled to collapse my chute in order to get down faster. The sudden silence was a shock. And it was bitterly cold.

"I landed gently in deep snow about one hundred yards from the Danube, and for a moment I stood there, temporarily dazed. Everything had happened so quickly.

"A Messerschmitt 109 roared towards me at an altitude of fifty feet. I apprehensively remembered tales of German pilots shooting bailed-out American flyers. I waited numbly for the thudding spray of bullets, but he ignored me. He banked sharply, and made two or three passes over the carcass of my B-24, *Consolidated Mess*, which had crashed on the opposite bank of the river.

"I got up slowly to look over the situation. There I was, plunked down in the heart of Germany in the middle of winter. I was alone on a large, snow-covered corn field. One or two miles to the south-west was a picturesque German village, nestling on the river. About a half mile behind were scattered bushes, insufficient for cover. Directly in front of me was the river. I was wearing a blue heated flying suit, O.D. coveralls, and thin-soled low shoes, encased in fleece-lined flying boots. Besides a wristwatch and the doubtful asset of my parachute, I had nothing of value; no escape kit, weapons, money, gloves, or cigarettes.

"Across the river, a group of curious villagers were pushing their way to the burning airplane. When they reached it, it started exploding with convulsive crackles, sending them scurrying. Meanwhile, another group of dark-clad figures was plunging through the snow in my direction. I stood quietly awaiting developments, since it seemed useless to try to run. When the leader was fifty yards away, he shouted to me, but I couldn't hear him. A bullet whistled over my head. I had seen enough war movies to know what to do now. Repressing a momentary impulse to laugh, I stuck my hands up over my head and yelled 'Kamerad!' In the approved melodramatic manner, a pistol was thrust into my back, and I was searched. Hoping for the best, I announced in my best German, 'Ich bin Amerikanische Offizier!' This didn't seem to impress my captors one way or the other. They seemed uniformly taciturn and surly. With a man on each side holding an arm, one man leading, and the rest following watchfully behind with their squirrel guns, I was firmly escorted to the village. I was a Prisoner of War."

From the Geneva Convention relative to the treatment of prisoners of war: Prisoners of war must at all times be humanely treated. Any unlawful act or omission by the Detaining Power causing death or seriously endangering the health of a prisoner of war in its custody is prohibited, and will be regarded as a serious breach of the present Convention. In particular, no prisoner of war may be subjected to physical mutilation or to medical or scientific experiments of any kind which are not justified by the medical, dental or hospital treatment of the prisoner concerned and carried out in his interest.

Likewise, prisoners of war must at all times be protected, particularly against acts of violence or intimidation and against insults and public curiosity. Measures of reprisal against prisoners of war are prohibited.

INTERROGATION

THE WELLINGTON in which Warrant Officer Douglas Connolly was flying what should have been the last operation of his tour with No. 149 Squadron as a Wireless Operator/Air Gunner, was shot down by flak over Bremerhaven on 27th August 1940. The crew baled out safely, were quickly rounded up and transported to Oberursel, a few miles west of Frankfurt am Main in central Germany. This was the site of Durchgangslager Luftwaffe (always known as Dulag Luft)—the combined transit camp and interrogation centre through which all captured fliers in the ETO passed on their way to prison camps. "No third degree or anything like that," said Connolly. "After a few days, they got fed up with hearing our number, rank and name, and moved us on. It was all fairly gentlemanly."

In those early days, fairly gentlemanly it was. There were three substantial barrack blocks, a cluster of wooden huts and a fifty-bed hospital nearby; a "permanent" staff of British officers, captured early in the war, occupied one of the barrack blocks and enjoyed such a life style that later prisoners in transit suspected them of treachery or worse. Certainly, for airmen such as Connolly, who stuck firmly to the rule (and his rights under the Geneva Convention) of giving no further information, his experience was typical—two days of interrogation and two or three waiting in the transit camp while a group was assembled for transport to an Offizierenlager (Oflag) or a Stammlager Luftwaffe (Stalag Luft). Later, as the air war escalated and the enemy grasped the need to learn the secrets of the latest Allied bombing aids, radar and armament, the atmosphere at Dulag Luft underwent a change. Any man who showed a sign of cracking under pressure would be interrogated until he was wrung dry.

In 1943, Navigator Eric Lapham remembered marching through the outskirts of Oberursel, and seeing "a collection of red-roofed half-timbered buildings gleaming in the sunlight. It was almost an idyllic setting . . . " Then the standard opening: "For you the war is over", the cigarette, the sympathy and pleasantries; then the smooth display of just how much was known about the airman's squadron, group, aircraft, personnel, equipment, even favourite pub and local dance hall. "It was the first time I'd heard that the Squadron lost four aircraft the night we were shot down," said Lapham.

Next, the questions, and perhaps a change of mood if the interrogator met resistance: the solitary cell, stifling hot by day and freezing cold at night, the absence of a toilet, the visit by the "Red Cross representative" who only wanted information in order to complete an "arrival report form" and assure your next-of-kin that you were safe.

Once that had been withstood, the atmosphere was likely to relax. There were books to read, cigarettes and food supplied by the Red Cross, a chance to wash and shave, and to write a letter home. From now on, the British flier was just another POW, photographed, numbered and recorded in Berlin. "I spent some time," wrote Lapham, "trying to make rank braid out of a piece of my shirt and a black shoe-lace, so as to present a more officer-like appearance."

Saved from the attentions of the mob by one of "Hitler's own", Bob Braham and Don Walsh soon found themselves at Dulag Luft, where they were stripped, searched again, and placed in separate cells for what by then was the standard fortnight stay. Their daily rations consisted of three slices of black bread and margarine with a bowl of thin soup. Two or three times a week, they were interrogated by Hauptmann Koch, and Braham was surprised at how much information about his RAF career the Hauptmann had on file. It was while he was in Dulag Luft that Braham learned of the award of his third DSO. "Koch brought a press cutting," he wrote, "from an English paper to my cell, saying 'Wing Commander, here is something you might like to keep. Your country thinks highly of you.' "

During one of his interrogations, Braham was introduced to the Luftwaffe pilot whose forty-fifth combat victim he had been. "He seemed friendly and shook hands, saying he was glad neither of us had been hurt. I gathered . . . he had lost his parents during one of the RAF's heavy raids on Hamburg, but he was quick to point out that he held no malice for me. 'It is the war,' he said."

And at their last session, Koch gave Braham the customary

propaganda line—that world Jewry was to blame for the war, and that it was not too late for Britain and Germany to settle their differences and unite against the Bolshevists. Braham doubted that the intelligence officer really believed all this himself. The two men joined a batch of POWs on the long train journey to Pomerania and the wide, wire-enclosed compounds of Stalag Luft III, Sagan, Silesia.

"In February 1945", recalled former P-51 pilot Walter Konantz, "I had just completed my combat tour with the 55th Fighter Group when I got a phone call from the replacement depot in northern England. It was my younger brother, Harold, who had just arrived in England as a replacement fighter pilot. I asked the 55th commander to call the depot and ask for Harold by name, which he did. I then volunteered to stay another month as an instructor in our 'Clobber College' check out program for newly arrived fighter pilots.

"The day before I was scheduled to leave for the states, Harold got shot down by a B-17 when he moved in close enough to identify the tail marking to see if they were the ones the 55th was to escort. He saw some smoke puffs from a side gun but never felt anything hit his plane. Within ten minutes his coolant temperature had pegged, steam was coming out of the cowling and the engine caught fire. He baled out and was captured as soon as he touched the ground.

"When he was finally taken to a Luftwaffe base for interrogation, he was asked his name and upon answering, the Luftwaffe officer shuffled through some papers, picked out one and studied it, then told him, 'We thought you had finished your tour and were on the way home.' He had some very up to date data on me!

"Harold had taken over my old P-51 and had not yet changed the first name of the pilot's name on the canopy rail."

Delmar Spivey, who was the SAO (Senior Allied Officer, Center Compound, Sagan) recalled: "most of our boys were interrogated at Dulag Luft, but others were less fortunate. Those who fell into the hands of the SS and the Gestapo were treated very badly before they were finally turned over, if they ever were, to custody of the Luftwaffe or the Wehrmacht. The great Fresnes prison in Paris was infamous for its treatment of POWs and political prisoners. Many of our men were able to escape after being shot down and to get into civilian clothes. If they were captured at a later date in civilian clothes they were then thrown into prison as spies. It usually took a long time to convince the men who ran these prisons that one was an American airman and not a spy. Nothing was too cruel for them to do to get these prisoners to talk. Some were sent to concentration camps, never to be heard from again. I recall the time when two British RAF officers who had been in Buchenwald came into our POW camp and discreetly gave the senior British officer, G.C.Kellett, the names of several USAAF officers languishing in that infamous concentration camp. Kellett gave me their names, and immediately every effort was made to persuade the Germans to release them. I do not know for certain that our efforts did any good, but I do know that one day these American prisoners came into our compound too frightened to talk. After they had been fed, rested, and reassured, they told us of the conditions at Buchenwald and drew us a picture of the whole establishment, including the death house and the house of forced prostitution. They had been there a long time and knew about the unbelievable things that went on; the organization that permitted the strong and ruthless prisoners to starve, beat, and kill their fellow men; the systematic starving and killing of tens of thousands of helpless people; the hopelessness of everyone there. Some of our gallant OSS men were there waiting their turn to march to that dreadful death house which later became so well known to the world.

"Contrary to that, the Luftwaffe treated most of us at Dulag Luft quite well. Usually, from ten days to two weeks after an airman was picked up he was through Dulag Luft and had rejoined his fellow POWs. Thereafter, thanks to the Red Cross and the YMCA, he was rather well fed, clothed, and housed. In my own case, once the Germans found out I wasn't going to talk and were quite sure I knew nothing, I was taken from the hospital to the nearby transient camp and turned loose in a large stockade filled with English and Americans. I reacted just like a trapped animal must feel when suddenly released. I didn't know whether to run or just stand there and admire all those dirty, unshaven, long-haired, half-naked airmen, bathing themselves in the warm August sun. For the first time in my life I knew the full meaning of the expression 'misery loves company.' I was lonesome and I wanted company."

A prominent visitor to Dulag Luft at Oberursel in 1941 was the German pilot, Franz von Werra, who had been captured after being shot down over England where he experienced the attentions of the British Air Interrogation Centre at Cockfosters, a similar operation to that of Dulag Luft. Following his stay with the British, he was incarcerated as a prisoner of war in Canada. He later managed an escape and a trek across the United States and down through Mexico before he was able to return to Germany via South America.

On his return, von Werra was ordered by Reichsmarschall Hermann Göring to visit all the POW in Germany where RAF airmen were being held, with particular attention to interrogation practices. He was unimpressed by the methods of Dulag Luft and informed Göring that he thought superficial. He stated that he would sooner be interviewed by a half dozen German interrogators than by one RAF expert. The Reichsmarschall responded positively to von Werra's official report on Dulag Luft, recommending various changes in procedures, and ordered the changes made. Many of von Werra's suggested changes to organization and methods were based on the British approach to prisoner interrogation.

In evaluating the approach and methods utilized by the Germans at Dulag Luft, the British had noted that the Germans cleverly altered the mood and atmosphere of the interrogations, disguising the adversarial element. So effective was this approach that, in many cases the exhausted prisoner, following a lengthy and helpful (to the Germans) interview, was left in confusion as to when the actual interrogation was going to start.

Typically, the interrogation experience of an arriving Allied airman at Dulag Luft began with the appearance of a supposed Red Cross representative, who came to the captive's cell and asked him to complete a long, official-looking form. The Red Cross person was a phoney and the form illegal. The method was just one of the ways the Germans used in an effort to gather additional information from new prisoners, beyond the name-rank-serial number they were obliged to provide by the rules of the 1929

Geneva Convention. When it became known in Britain and the U.S. that the Germans were using this practice, the Allies protested and the Red Cross reference was discontinued, but the form was still used.

In such sessions, the majority of prisoners gave only the legally required data, and simply ignored all further questions on the form, many of which related to their military units and operations. In fact, the Germans expected such behaviour and attached more importance to what they believed they were learning about their prisoner's personality. They looked for vulnerabilities, weaknesses and other characteristics that might be exploited later. They noted impressions about the man's level of self-confidence, his personal habits, and whether he seemed responsive to praise or encouragement. They sometimes reacted with feigned disappointment when a prisoner became adamant about not giving any information, and explained to him the vital importance of their being able to prove that the prisoner was, in fact, an Allied airman and not a spy. They then alluded to the much less humane methods of the Gestapo in obtaining information from Allied prisoners, and the Luftwaffe camp staff's interest in saving prisoners from such a fate. They called attention to the commonality of honour among air officers and, in the context of the Gestapo threat, again stressed with urgency the importance of fully confirming the prisoner's identity through his revealing his flying unit.

The environment of the prisoner at Dulag Luft was intentionally oppressive. The unease of the captive was exploited by his jailors, who used methods such as manipulating the temperature in his tiny five-foot by ten-foot prison cell. By making the little room unbearably hot the Germans almost guaranteed an attitude of thankfulness, relief and appreciation in the prisoner when he was finally allowed out of the sweltering room, if only for the respite of another session of questioning. The Germans, of course, claimed that the excessive temperatures were due to breakdowns in the heating system. The 'heat treatment', coupled with being confined to a tiny cell with only a bed and one electric light that was turned on and off randomly from somewhere outside the cell, and a little window that was painted over, could be very effective.

By the time of the prisoner's second interrogation session, the thoughts, comments, and notes of his initial interrogator had been given to another questioner; a specialist selected for his expertise in dealing with either bomber crewmen or fighter pilots.

All the Dulag Luft interrogators were fluent in English, many of them having lived for a time in England or the United States. In their own ways they were skilled psychologists, keen observers of human behaviour who had developed particular techniques for use on their aviator guests. Mostly, they concentrated on befriending, flattering and relaxing their captives, softening the atmosphere with the offer of little comforts like cigarettes, chocolate, and light conversation incorporating interests such as literature, music, or sports, aspects they had discovered about their subject. All such practices were geared towards making the prisoner feel safer in the strange new environment of confinement in a foreign land.

These techniques were relatively effective on some prisoners, breaking down their resolve not to give any information other than name, rank and service number. Some reports about the POW experience indicate that officers, through their backgrounds and training, were somewhat more susceptible to the conversational techniques of the specialist interrogators. They were often more easily drawn into dialogue or debate with their questioners, than were the majority of enlisted prisoners.

Typically, of the ten men that made up an American heavy bomber crew, four were officers and six were sergeant gunners. Most of the sergeant airmen saw no reason to engage in conversation with the interrogators. They were less susceptible to the sort of talk that more often drew the officers into chats which, unknowingly to the prisoners, resulted in seemingly insignificant buts of information passing to their captors. Thus, in the view of the Germans, the officers were riper targets for their attentions.

Normally, the patience of the German interrogators began to wear down when, after several unproductive sessions, it was clear that the subject would simply not respond satisfactorily to the friendly approach. At that point the interrogator would return to the Gestapo threat theme, making much of the implied violence that was to be expected if a prisoner continued to withhold information about his squadron or group. After all, short of such information, it was impossible to positively establish that the prisoner was actually a flier rather than a spy.

Too, without such information, no notification of his capture and safety could be sent out to the International Red Cross who would then notify the prisoner's family. This was calculated to raise the anxiety of the prisoner, who knew that by then, his relatives would have been told that he was missing in action, but not that he was alive and well. The fear was multiplied with the realization that until notification was received by the Red Cross, he could be killed or spirited away somewhere by the Germans and held for who knew how long, while his captors denied ever having taken him prisoner. The Germans played on every potential fear they could. When they found that a prisoner had relatives living in German-occupied territory, they rolled out threats about what might happen if the prisoner continued to resist cooperating. Threats of various types were made, though rarely acted upon. The interrogators of the Dulag Luft center were generally above violence and held a condescending view of Gestapo tactics, priding themselves on their ability to extract the desired information without resorting to such vulgarity. Threats though, were well within their remit.

For most of a prisoner's stay at the Dulag Luft camp, he was subjected to the more friendly, considerate approach by his interrogators, who mainly believed in the concept that one can catch more flies with honey than with vinegar. Putting a prisoner off balance through the offer of little favours achieved much, as they saw it, even if no specific information was forthcoming from the prisoner. It was usually enough to manoeuvre the prisoner into feeling that he was at least slightly indebted to the interrogator, a debt that might be called in at a later time.

A phenomenon common to most of the airmen who sat out some of the war as guests of Stalag Luft I or Stalag Luft III was the sense, belief even, that they had been through and left the interrogation experience of Dulag Luft without ever having given their inquisitors a single shred of useful information. Most, too, were astonished by the amount of accurate information their German captors already had about the organization, units, and operations of the British and American air forces.

The philosphy of Hanns Scharff, the primary interrogator of Allied fighter pilots at Dulag Luft, was essentially that decent and humane treatment of prisoners achieved the desired results. It also improved the image of the German captor in the view of the civilized world.

When Scharff learned one evening in November 1944 that the legendary Hubert 'Hub' Zemke, leader of the highly successful 56th Fighter Group of the USAAF, had arrived at Oberursel and was already in the Cooler, Scharff hurried over to meet the man he knew of as 'the great Hun-hater.' He had come to think of Zemke as a brilliant combat leader and air fighter, and admired the American's reputation as an intellectual, steeped in management and diplomatic skills. Still, Scharff harboured a few doubts about the man and wondered if he was really that special.

Scharff had a favourite ploy that he used on certain new arrivals at the Oberursel camp. He would show a photo of some of the new man's squadron mates and then deliberately incorrectly identify one of the group. The new arrival would sometimes rise to the bait and rebuff Scharff, correctly naming the man in the picture. He doubted that such a ruse would work on Zemke.

When they met, Scharff showed Colonel Zemke some American newspapers headlining recent Allied losses; he also showed him some German papers touting Nazi successes. He then attempted to confuse the American with a photo showing Zemke with five other pilots of his group. The picture had been taken in the officer's club at Zemke's base only five days before he had been shot down.

Scharff's admiration of Zemke and the Colonel's leadership skills grew as they talked. He liked the American and suggested through channels that Zemke be made Senior Allied Officer of one of the prisoner of war camps, the recently established Stalag Luft I, at Barth on the Baltic coast. Many of Zemke's fellow officers and pilots were already interned at Barth. So impressed was Scharff with Hub Zemke, that he did all he could in the way of favours to make the American's time at Dulag Luft as comfortable as possible, in the circumstances.

author's note: Both Hanns Scharff and Hub Zemke passed away in 1994.

From the Geneva Convention relative to the treatment of Prisoners of War: Each party to a conflict must issue an identity card to every person under its jurisdiction liable to become a PW showing name, rank, serial number, and date of birth. When questioned a PW is bound only to provide this information. Physical or mental torture or any other form of coercion to secure information of any kind whatever is prohibited. Effects and articles of personal use (aside from military equipment, arms or ammunition) are to remain in the PW's possession. However, currency and other items of value may be taken on order of an officer after issuance of a receipt. PWs shall be promptly evacuated from the combat zone to camps for their detention.

FELLOW KRIEGIES

PERHAPS THE PRINCIPAL DIFFERENCE between a convict in a civil gaol and a prisoner-of-war in the hands of the enemy is the time factor; the convict can look forward to release within a certain period and, given good behavior, he may expect to serve less than his original sentence. The POW has no such guarantee—the length of his sentence is determined only by the duration of the war.

To pass the months in limbo while your buddies were getting all the glory was no fun at all.

When Eric Lapham arrived at Stalag Luft III in July 1943, the accommodation ratio of eight men to a room was commodious compared with what it would become as the intensifying battle in the skies of Europe engendered an ever-growing stream of unwilling residents. Within three months, Lapham had twelve mess-mates in the Centre Camp. "One man was a first generation American of Canadian parents; he had been employed as an illustrator in the Disney studios in Hollywood. When he was offered transfer to a mess in one of the newly formed American blocks, he privately opined that, while he was proud to be an American, he found it difficult to accept them in the mass. His compatriot, an inveterate crap player, was completely opposite, and could not get away fast enough."

Numbers inevitably continued to grow, and by January 1945, when the camp was under warning for the westward march, eighteen men were sharing Lapham's room. Their three-tiered bunks were narrow, and a restless sleeper was liable to suffer an eight-foot fall onto the concrete floor if he turned over in the same direction twice.

Burt Joseph's first encounter with his fellow Kriegies was at Obermassfeld, some 30 miles north of Schweinfurt in Thuringia. Originally a boy's school, then a Hitler Youth camp, Obermassfeld had been converted into a hospital for Allied POWs. "It was staffed," Joseph recorded, "by members of the British Royal Army Medical Corps who had been captured at Dunkirk, in Crete and in Africa. Although they were eligible for repatriation under the

Geneva Convention, they chose to stay in order to treat the ever-increasing stream of wounded prisoners."

Joseph had good reason to be grateful for the selfless dedicationof those unsung heroes of the RAMC, for "without the skill of an Australian plastic surgeon, it is likely that I would have remained one of those horribly disfigured scarfaces who came out of the war." (Almost fifty years later, in St. Augustine, Florida, Joseph at last succeeded in tracking down that skilful surgeon. Major John Sherman MBE was then "ninety years old, almost blind, hard of hearing, but very much with it".)

Joseph also found a stabilizing influence in the stoicism of his fellow patients, particularly that of Captain John Arundell who, although gravely ill with tuberculosis—a condition incurred during two years spent in a Nazi dungeon—was "a never-failing spirit and as serene an individual as I ever encountered." Sadly, that brave officer died shortly after his return to England on repatriation. He was, as Joseph later established, the 16th and last Lord Arundell of Wardour.

Of his arrival at Stalag Luft 1, Barth, Don Ackerson recalled: ". . . we were greeted at the gates by a bunch of Kriegies calling out 'you'll be sorry' and 'hard luck'. This was to be our home for many months. It was an officer camp with a lot of British at that time. Some of them had been in since the war started. One had been in since before the war. He had been shot down on a reconnaissance flight before the declaration of war. Some of the old Kriegies were 'around the bend,' a term meaning crazy."

John Hurd's reception was efficient and instantly hygienic: clothes were fumigated, bodies were showered and heads were shaved; faces were photographed and POW numbers allocated. The camp consisted of single-storey barrack blocks, each with a wash-room (in which the prisoners contrived to do some basic cooking), and rows of two-tier bunks. Hurd found a bunk next to the wash-room and beside a window, through which, after lights-out, he could gaze up at the stars. There were daily head-counts and regular checks of photographs and numbers.

For America, Britain and the European nations (but not the Soviet Union), the rules which governed the treatment of POWs were laid down in an international convention signed at Geneva in 1929. The signatory governments agreed that all prisoners should be humanely treated; they were not to be required to give their captors any information other than their service number or their rank and name (the general belief that all three were obligatory was a misconception); they were to be permitted to retain their clothes and personal possessions; POW camps were to be located away from battle zones, and each was to be equipped with a hospital; the standard of the prisoners' rations and of their accommodation should equate with that provided for the captor nation's non-combatant troops. They were entitled to receive mail from home, which could include food, books and clothing.

According to the Convention, POWs could not be required to undertake work that was dangerous, unhealthy or helpful to the captor nation's war effort, nor to work for overly long hours; warrant and non-commissioned officers could only be employed in supervisory duties, and commissioned officers could not be required to work at all. While POWs were subject to the captor nation's laws, and could be penalized for disciplinary offences committed in the camps, they were neither to be given corporal punishment nor put in squalid cells. Even for escaping, the maximum penalty on recapture was solitary confinement for thirty days.

"To live in the same clothes for months and months," wrote Frank Kautzmann, "almost forgetting the simple pleasure of changing into something laundered; and to go without a bath or a shave— these things, these simple things weigh down on me."

The matter of dress was seen rather differently by Wing Commander Lewis Hodges (later Air Chief Marshal Sir Lewis), when he was commanding No. 161 Squadron. "No," he told his officers (and it will never now be known if his tongue was in his cheek), "No, I could never walk into a prison camp without a tunic. I mean, they wouldn't know what rank I was".

Kenneth Simmons, in Kriegie, describes an Appell, and a typical barracks organization (his own on his arrival at Sagan): "The official German count could not begin until the Commandant had arrived to witness it. When the Commandant arrived, Colonel Spivey called the entire compound to attention and saluted. The

Commandant ordered the count to be taken and we were again given 'at ease.' That was when I first saw Pop-eye.

"Pop-eye was the top German sergeant of Sagan's Center Compound and he practically ran the camp. We called him Pop-eye because he had only one eye, and he was as tough as nails. He was nearly six feet tall, stout, and had black hair. He would scream and bellow as the guards proceeded to each block to make the official German count. There were two German corporals assigned to our block, and they would always foul up the count. One would go down the front ranks counting noses, and the other would go down the rear rank counting butts. We named the front rank Corporal Dumbkoff, and the rear rank Corporal Shisenkoff.

When all other blocks had reported to Pop-eye, Dumbkoff and Shisenkoff were still counting. 'Ein, zwei, drei, vier,' they counted as Pop-eye appeared. He put Dumbkoff in a brace, and 'ate his butt out good.' Dumbkoff really got on the ball and concluded the count. Pop-eye proceeded to the Commandant to report the official count."

". . . each combine has a group of fuehrers. I am the bread fuehrer, and I issue your bread every morning after breakfast. We get six thin slices of bread per day by slicing forty slices to the loaf. I am an artist, and it's not easy to do. You can eat the bread any time you want, but most of us eat two slices at each meal. Pirtle is the coffee fuehrer and he makes all the coffee. He keeps it under his bed and rations the strength and amount of coffee according to our supply. If we have an abundant supply he makes it stronger. Rhinehart is food fuehrer. He is in charge of all parcels except the coffee. He is also in charge of any German rations. He plans all meals and helps the new cooks prepare their food. He will also teach you two how to cook. Clark is the combine fuehrer. He is in command of the combine, and has the final say in all matters. If you have any gripes about anything, take them to Clark. You will never question the decision of a fuehrer. Each of us was elected by the popular vote of the combine to serve six months. A fuehrer can be removed by a secret ballot of seven members of the combine."

From the Geneva Convention relative to the treatment of prisoners of war: Article 21 authorizes internment and provides for the release on parole or promise if allowed by the law of the PWs own nation. Parole release may not be imposed involuntarily. Parolees are bound on their personal honor to fulfill the terms and conditions of their parole. Close confinement is not authorized except for conditions of health. Article 22 requires internment only on land and not in unhealthy areas. PWs are to be assembled in camps according to nationality, language and customs. Article 23 prohibits the sending of or detention of PWs in combat zones.

THE GUARDS

THE BRITISH PILOT Robert Kee came to believe that there were two Germanys: "The Wehrmacht Germany which saluted you when it passed you in the camp and allowed you to write home three times a month, and the SS Germany which beat you in the stomach with lengths of hosepipe and shot you in the early morning."

The regime at Stalag Luft III, Sagan, however austere it was, could not be described as harsh. Some of the staff were venal, some were inefficient, and some were sympathetic, if not actually friendly. The prisoners were quick to take advantage of any weakness— sometimes by apparent affability, sometimes by bribery and subsequently blackmail—to suborn their captors and pursue their private battle with the enemy.

So strict was rationing in Germany from 1942 onwards, that private soldiers were restricted to three cigarettes a day, and it was hard for a camp guard who enjoyed the weed to decline the offer of a packet in return for some small service. So the thin end of the wedge was introduced.

After the Great Escape in March 1944, for which the German Commandant and ten of his officers were arraigned at a court martial, the evidence against them was overwhelming in its detail. Recording the fact that every prisoner, on arrival at the camp, received a bed and a palliasse, a knife, fork and spoon, a dish and a coffee cup, two blankets, three sheets and a towel, it revealed that, in the last fifteen months, an extraordinary number of articles had simply disappeared, including 1,699 blankets, 3,424 towels, 655 palliasses, 1,212 bolsters, 34 chairs, 62 tables, 76 benches, 90 beds, 246 watering cans, 1,219 knives, 582 forks, 408 spoons, 69 lamps and 30 shovels. "While German families who had lost all," the summary of evidence continued, "could only receive replacement in the most needy circumstances, the imprisoned 'terror airmen' lived among the things entrusted to them in almost devilish ways and with them constantly continued the war against the Reich behind the barbed wire, and with success."

One camp guard who would always be remembered by inmates of Stalag Luft III, and not altogether unfondly, was Oberfeldwebel Glemnitz. The one-time POW adjutant, Squadron leader D. M.

Strong (whose initials brought him the nickname "DIM"), rose after the war to the rank of Air Vice-Marshal. Inspecting the RAF station at Gatow in 1963, he recognised a civilian who was working on the base. "Hello, Mr. Strong," said Glemnitz and, glancing at the wealth of gold braid, added "See how well I trained you!"

"Most POWs had little contact," wrote Eric Lapham, "with the German personnel. In fact, we were expected to avoid contact with the guards and ferrets, and report any approaches from them. There was common dislike of 'Slim', the corporal with the party powers. 'Slim' was short for 'slimy', and he was so referred to, to his face. Contact was left to those best equipped for the task, and normally with a definite aim. There were some amazing cases of blackmail to secure ink, pens, photographic paper and the like".

Notices beside the inner wire, dire as they might be, were not devoid of a certain comic element. "Danger of Life! We shoot!" they read at Heydekrug, "We shoot without warning or call whenever you touch or surpass wire or pole!" And at Thorn "Halt! Trespassing of warning wire means death!" At Wolfsberg, "Do not approach the warning wire or it will be shot!"

Each evening at Stalag Luft III, the guards made their nightly bed-check rounds shortly after the lights in the barracks had been turned off. In the course of the continuing campaign to harass their German captors, many American airmen took part in a form of what they called "goon-baiting."

In the pitch-blackness of a barracks block, the men would be engaged in a range of demanding pursuits. Some sat reading, with others in intense concentration over a chess board. At a table four kriegies were involved in a poker game, while to one side of the room a man sat mending his clothing, and another nearby was writing a letter. As he began moving through the darkness, one guard invariably shined his flashlight around the room, resulting in catcalls, wisecracks and obscenities shouted at the confused German, as the Americans squinted and shaded their eyes at 'the glare.' They complained to the guard for making it so bright in the room that they couldn't get any work done.

The relationships between the prisoners and the guards could be complicated. While relatively few of the inmates spoke more than a few words of German, some of the guards were fluent in English and, over time, a number of guarded 'friendships' developed, all definitely against the policies of both the German and Allied camp administrators. The policies, however, were violated with regularity, if only to enable the occasional brief conversation or the giving of a cigarette or cup of coffee to a guard. Functionally, some of these relationships were based on the guard or prisoner, or both, acting as contacts for their respective organizations, obtaining and providing information. The Germans used guards in some situations to get information about escape-related activity. The POWs cosied up to certain guards who were open to taking favours in exchange for items or information the prisoners needed. It was a two-way street, generally discouraged by both administrations, but also exploited by both.

Eighth Air Force bombardier Kenneth Simmons recalled: "During the early hours of Monday, November 13, a heavy snow began to fall, forming a solid white coat over the grounds of Sagan. By dawn the white coat of snow lay several inches deep and the temperature continued to drop.

"Chief ferret Rhoder entered the Center Compound early with a staff of twenty specialists and the entire German guard of the Center Compound. He spoke to Pop-eye for several minutes, outlining his plan in detail. Pop-eye barked out orders placing his guards at every entrance to every barracks in the compound. Pop-eye personally checked every guard under his command, and ordered the bugler to sound appell.

"Promptly at eight o'clock, Rhoder ordered every barracks to stand by for a search. He was extremely cocky as he marched down the aisle of our barracks while we dressed. He loved the element of surprise, and he thought he had caught us off guard. But our Intelligence had paid one of Rhoder's men fifty packs of cigarettes for the tip-off about this search, and we were ready.

"We were lined up in a column of two's as soon as we finished dressing. Four guards stood at each door and each of us was thoroughly searched from head to foot as we passed through to the parade ground. A fifth guard stood outside, and counted us as we came out. When all the barracks were empty the ferrets totalled the count, at each barracks door, for the appell. Pop-eye moved all prisoners to the parade ground, and placed guards on he outer edges of the perimeter track to keep us there.

"I noticed that four guards were placed outside at the four corners of each barracks. Rhoder divided his twenty specialists into five teams, and the search began. Closets were emptied, beds were removed, and pally-asses (sic) were gutted. Kitchens were taken apart piece by piece, and food parcels were checked item by item. Floor boards were removed and examined for possible tunnel entrances. Several sections of walls were ripped out in every barracks in search of possible hidden weapons.

"When the inside search was completed, the search teams moved outside. They checked the barracks roof, attic, foundations, and outside walls. Several sections of outside walls were torn loose and checked. All of the loot was loaded on two wagons Rhoder had brought into the compound.

"From the barracks the search continued to the latrines, kitchens, library, and auditorium. Rhoder had several men dip buckets attached to ropes into the latrine holes to check for hidden articles. He went over the Center Compound with a fine tooth comb examining everything he could think of. He had made a list of places he had apparently failed to check before, and he checked off the list as his men completed the search. He hunted madly for tunnels after all the buildings had been searched. He made three special trips back to the latrines, library, and auditorium. He must have stayed in the auditorium for an hour. The search lasted for four and one-half hours.

"During all of this time we stood in dozens of small groups talking, smoking, and moving around trying to keep warm. The snow continued to fall, and all of us grew anxious, nervous, and tense as the search failed to end. Those responsible for vitally important projects and secret material suffered agonies as the minutes slowly passed by. Hundreds of hopeful hearts anxiously awaited the end of the search, to learn if a month's, six month's, or even year's work had been in vain.

"The Germans never failed to uncover a few hidden weapons, tools, and documents, but this was because we always placed them where the Germans would be sure to find them. The German ferrets had to find something for the camp Commandant, and the quicker they found a few saws, shovels, knives, and misleading secret documents, the quicker the search would end. We saved valuable equipment by making sure they would find enough junk to satisfy their Nazi ego. We did everything possible during a search to make the Germans believe they were superior in wit, and it paid off in big dividends.

"Preparing valuable equipment for a search was of great importance. It was the responsibility of Intelligence to hide this equipment so the ferrets would not find it. Some of it was placed in sight of the search teams. Radio tubes were placed in the center of a roll of toilet paper, and the toilet paper was left on top of the clothes locker. Some small tools and weapons were placed inside of GI shoes in the closets. Other items were left in open view of the ferrets. The most valuable items had to be hidden where they could not be found. Closets were rebuilt with false bottoms. The Nazis never thought of tearing a closet to pieces, since their carpenters had built them. Stoves were reworked with secret compartments, and the concrete foundations for the barracks stoves were hollowed out by expert masons. Many items were buried on the parade ground the Sunday night before the search. They never thought of digging up the parade ground. It was surprising how many items they would miss that were actually in plain sight. Major Thompson once said that the only radio equipment ever destroyed was a receiver set hidden in a pasteboard box, which was crushed by a German ferret when he sat down to rest.

"Finally Rhoder came out from under the auditorium, and blew his whistle. The search was over, and all discovered items were taken by the search teams to the two wagons. Clark, Pirtle, and I joined several hundred prisoners who had gathered about the wagons to see how much the Germans had found. Rhoder always allowed us to get a good look, to show us that he was the smartest man in Sagan. When we gathered about the two wagons, I got another surprise. Special actors stepped forward to their utter amazement while others flattered Rhoder and his assistants about how he had outsmarted us. While they kidded Rhoder and worked him into a stage of hysteria, sleight of hand artists stole dozens of articles from the wagons, and passed them through the crowded ranks.

"During this repossessing process, I saw one of the boldest acts ever tried at Sagan. David Bowling, one of the actors, waited until the ferrets started bragging and boasting of their cleverness. He suddenly rushed forward, slapped Rhoder's assistant on the back, grabbed a large folder of maps, and walked through the crowd to the barracks. Bowling passed ten German guards with the bundle under his arm, yet not one of them ever dreamed that he was carrying loot from their wagons. I decided that the bolder the act, the greater the chance for success.

"When Rhoder finally assembled his twenty detectives and prepared them for departure, nearly one-third of our possessions had been regained without his slightest suspicion.

"Late in the afternoon, Captain McGee announced that projects Dave and George were both safe, and that we had lost only what we had intended to lose. He also informed us that forty-seven items had been repossessed from the wagons.

"All of us were exhausted and half frozen from the long search, but very happy over the results. I had never been around so many clever men in my life. I decided that Kriegie Intelligence and strategy could not be equalled anywhere in the world.

"During the next three nights, Rhoder launched full scale surprise raids on nearly every barracks in the compound, in an attempt to uncover something that would lead to Dave. Since the news had been suspended, every attempt failed. Sad faces and grouchy dispositions convinced Rhoder that his Kriegies had lost their secret news agency. He finally gave up his overtime night activities.

"On Friday, November 17, at the usual time, the readers of Dave resumed their old duties, and the news began once again in the compound. Mott handed three men a book to look at, and Pirtle dealt six hands of poker, as the reader joined our table. He concluded with a message from Colonel Spivey: 'Congratulations on your excellent cooperation and efficiency during the search. You displayed fine teamwork after the search, and recovered much property. Most important of all, not one single major project was discovered.'

"We sat at our combine table for the full allotted ten minutes discussing the news of the war's progress. All members of the combine were the happiest I had seen them since I came to Sagan. Adding to the success of the search just completed, many old prisoners said it was the best week they had experienced since they had been captured."

"The treatment at Stalag 17B, Krems, was never considered good," according to Bob Doherty, a tail gunner with the 96th Bomb Group stationed at Snetterton Heath, England, "and was at times even brutal. An example of extreme brutality occurred in early 1944. Two men attempting to escape were discovered in an out-of-bounds area adjoining the compound. As soon as they were discovered, they threw up their hands indicating their surrender. They were shot while their hands were raised. One of the men died immediately, but the other was only injured in the leg. After he fell a guard ran to within 20 feet of him and fired again. The guards then turned toward the barracks and fired wild shots in that direction. One shot entered a barrack and seriously wounded an American who was lying in his bunk. Permission was denied the Americans by the Germans to bring the body of the dead man into the compound for burial, and medical treatment for the injured man in the outer zone was delayed several hours.

"One POW was mentally sick when he was taken to the hospital where no provisions were made to handle cases of this type. In a moment of insanity the POW jumped from a window and ran to the fence, followed by a French doctor and orderlies who shouted to the guard not to shoot him. The patient was dressed in hospital pajamas which should have indicated to the guard that he was mentally unbalanced even if the doctor had not called the warning. As the patient climbed over the fence, the guard shot him in the heart.

"There were about 30 recorded cases of guards striking POWs with bayonets, pistols and a rifle butt. Protests to the commandant were always useless. In fact, on one occasion the commandant is reported to have stated that men were lucky to get off so lightly.

"On another occasion, an order was issued that all POWs take everything that they wanted to keep and stand on the parade ground as if they were leaving camp. Nothing was touched in the barracks during the search that ensued. The same procedure was followed on the next day, and still nothing was touched. The third day, most of the POWs left behind many articles of food, clothing and comfort equipment. On this occasion, the German troops entered the compound with wagons and took away any and all articles left in the barracks during the parade. The Protecting Power described this act as plunder to the German commandant who finally promised to return the items, but this proved to be an almost impossible task."

From the Geneva Convention relative to the treatment of prisoners of war: One of the most important chapters in the Convention is that relating to penal and disciplinary sanctions (Articles 82-108). One key principle is that detainees are subject to the laws, regulations and orders in force for the detaining power's armed forces. This chapter sets forth the circumstances under which PWs may be tried for various infractions of the laws and regulations of the detaining power; establishes maximum punishments for disciplinary offenses including attempted escapes; provides specific safeguards and guarantees of a fair judicial proceeding; and prohibits procedures and punishments contrary to those set out in the Convention.

MEAL TIMES

IT IS USUALLY THE WAY with any group of people who are cooking for themselves that, while it is OK to criticise the variety or quantity available, it is not permissible to criticise the cook. This was a rule which navigator Flying Officer Bobby Stark, an Ulsterman whose parachute descent from a crippled Halifax bomber ended on a garage roof in Holland, happened to infringe one November evening in 1943 at Stalag Luft III.

"Within minutes," he recorded, "I was appointed cook—a job which was to be mine until the evening of January 28th 1945, when the Germans evacuated the camp on reports that a Russian tank unit had crossed the Oder at Steinau about 45 miles from the camp.

"Breakfast normally consisted of ersatz coffee and three thin slices of black bread with margarine or butter. Lunch comprised a bowl of kohlrabi soup or barley cooked in water and two slices of bread—all provided by the goons. It was impossible to improve the soup, but the 'barleygoo' tasted a little more interesting if mixed with a spoonful of dried milk powder. Afternoon tea in the English tradition was served at four o'clock—two slices of bread covered with honey or jam and occasionally a foul-tasting blood sausage paste.

"Two rooms shared a small coal stove and oven for forty minutes in the afternoon and a further thirty minutes in the evening to heat up the dishes. Pots and baking dishes were manufactured from empty Klim tins by a group of 'tin-bashers'.

"The cook's chief responsibility was dinner, the main meal of the day. The Germans provided two small potatoes per man per day, a vegetable in season came from Liffy's garden, and the meat or fish from the Red Cross parcels. The Canadian or American parcels usually contained small tins of spam, corned beef and salmon. The cook had to think up different ways of serving whatever was available. The salmon was the basis of my most successful menu: I drained the water off three tins and placed the salmon in a dish with a little butter. A sauce of thick powdered milk and grated cheese was poured over the fish, the dish was covered, heated in the oven for about thirty minutes, and served with boiled potatoes. Every three weeks this was followed by a chocolate pudding, made from ground black bread crusts, raisins, currants and prunes, mixed with margarine, powdered milk, sugar and a precious bar of chocolate. The pudding was cooked and served with 'cream' made from a thick beaten mix of Klim and water. I was always surprised when my mess-mates were able to get out of bed next morning."

"Food. It all comes back to food." So wrote Frank Kautzmann as he sat in his prison block near Nuremberg on 3rd March 1945. "I can describe in the most minute detail the appearance and taste of any food that I've ever enjoyed. I can almost taste chocolate ice cream as it melts on my tongue. I can see the steam rise up as I cut through a Thanksgiving sweet potato with my cold fork. I can smell a fresh pie baking in the kitchen. I can feel the burn on my fingers as I reach for fresh cookies before they're cooled. I could describe my life in food terms . . ."

"Prison camp food required a lot of imagination and a great deal of ingenuity," recalls Don Ackerson. "There were a number of POW artisans who were sheet metal workers and made pans to order and fans to get air into the tunnels. We had all sorts of pans made out of the cans that came in the Red Cross parcels and the powdered milk cans (Klim) were used to make air pipes for the escape tunnels. But food was the one pleasure we had. Here are some of the recipes:

MEAT PIE (serves 4)
1/2 can luncheon meat (Spam)
1 can 'C' ration stew
1 can cheese
1 box K-2 biscuits or 1/2 box cereal
Klim (powdered milk)
Make a crust by mixing ground up crackers, dry Klim, sugar, salt, and melted margarine. Bake crust til dry. Then put in one slice of Spam and one slice of cheese on top of the Spam. Heat the stew with some Klim and half of the can of cheese until the mixture is fairly thin and the cheese is melted. Then pour over the Spam and cheese, cover with crust and bake til the crust is brown.

CHOCOLATE PIE (serves 4)
3 squares of 'D' bar

20 squares of sugar
3/4 can of Klim (mixed thick) and
pie crust as above.
Make the usual pie crust and bake. Grind up the chocolate and mix with sugar and Klim. Boil 4 or 5 minutes til sugar is good and melted and chocolate is dissolved. Put in crust and bake until good and firm.

PEANUT BUTTER PIE (serves 8)
crackers or cereal
Klim
1/4 lb sugar
1/4 can peanut butter
salt
shortening
Make regular Kriegie crust and bake. Mix about 1/2 can of Klim with 1/4 to 1/2 box of cereal and 1/4 lb of sugar. Heat and boil until the sugar is blended. Take off the fire and cool slightly and blend in the peanut butter. Beat until the mixture is blended well, pour into the crust and bake until stiff.

KRIEGIE CAKE (CHOCOLATE RAISIN) (serves 4)
2 boxes K-2 crackers or 1 1/2 boxes of cereal
Klim
Sugar
Raisins
4 squares of 'D' bar
baking powder or bicarb pills
Grind up crackers until good and powdery (do the same with the cereal). Put in about 4 heaping tablespoons of sugar and a pinch of salt. Add baking powder (1 tablespoon or 8 ground up bicarb pills). Melt chocolate with mixed Klim and add to mixture with enough milk to make the mixture thin enough to resemble cake batter. Mix in some raisins (or prunes). Bake until done.

MEAT LOAF
1 or 2 cans of corned beef
1 can of liver paté
Klim
salt

1 or 2 ground up K-2 crackers
Mix the corned beef in a bowl with milk until the paté can be blended in evenly. Add salt and mix in the ground-up crackers. The mixture can be kneaded and rolled into a loaf. Bake until brown with a slice of onion on top if you're lucky enough to have an onion.

KRIEGIE DEVILS FOOD CAKE (serves 4)
1 1/2 cups flour (cereal or ground up K-2 biscuits)
1 teaspoon soda (10 bicarb pills)
1/2 teaspoon salt
1/2 cup shortening (butter or margarine)
1 1/2 cups sugar
2 squares baker's chocolate
1 cup milk
Grind cereal up fine with a cup or roller. Add soda and salt. Cream butter, add sugar gradually and cream together til light and fluffy. Add melted chocolate and blend. Add flour alternatively with milk, blending all the time to keep the mixture even and uniform. Put in a greased pan and bake in a hot oven (as hot as we can get it) for 1 1/2 hours.

"We all took turns cooking and dividing up the rations. None of it ever went to waste, even the failures. Cooking was a problem because of the scarcity of fuel which was coal. The cook stoves would take any hard fuel and were also used to heat the rooms. Since the parcels had prunes or raisins in them, some groups made prune and raisin brew. This was a mixture which was allowed to ferment in a crock. When good and fermented, it was strained and drunk. A little bit of alcohol went a long way and the morning after brought the worst sick hangover in memory. Our room combine valued the prunes and raisins too much to use them in such a poisonous way!"

The main meal for NCO prisoners at Sagan was produced in the cookhouse by thirty volunteers, whose work was demanding but gave them access (or so the other prisoners believed) to more and better food. For other meals, each hut was equipped with a stove, a hot-plate and an oven.

The diet at Stalag 17B, Krems, was meagre—barley-mash, potatoes or rutabagas, with a ration of dark bread and an occasional sausage. The prisoners at Krems relied a lot on the regular delivery of Red

Cross parcels. "Home for Easter, chaps," said a room-mate. "The goons have absolutely had it," Watching him take two slices of bread and dig his knife into a tin of jam, Kee was about to remonstrate. "Then I remembered that we weren't on half parcels any more so it didn't really matter if he took too much, but it was difficult to get out of the habit of minding."

Luther Cox, a B-24 navigator who was shot down on 19th January 1943, recalls: "Food. As the months and years go by, that word assumes more and more significance. These eight POWs pooled their Red Cross parcels and the smattering of German food given us. We had no pots or pans so the first thing on the schedule was to figure out how to get some. We were quite dismayed to find out that there were none, at least, we had none. It was the responsibility of each mess unit to make their own pots and pans. With the willing help of the older Kriegies (those captured earlier, thus longer in the bag), we started opening the seams of old tin cans and flattened them into sheets. These sheets were in turn fastened to each other by seaming them; by crimping their edges together. These larger sheets were then shaped into the forms of desired pans. Most of the pans were about ten inches by eight inches and three or four inches deep. A pan of this type could be used for just about everything, from stew to cake. The first numbers of pans remained in the prototype category, a fancy word for just passable. However, later we grew in experience; which meant that we had fewer cuts and smashed fingers and the pan would hold together even under a load and heat.

Like anything else, there were always tricks to the trade. Some Kriegies simply could not make one that would do the job, while there were others who made them look almost store bought. Well, at least they looked pretty good and did the job. Tin foil from the British cigarettes was used to solder the joints. They even held water, eventually. Little blow torches were made and grease was put in them to make fuel. Some of the Kriegies who became very talented in this endeavor turned out masterpieces, such as double boilers, pitchers, etc. For the entire block (building) there was just one stove to cook on. This stove had a surface top area of about six feet by four feet. The portion that really got hot the best was obviously much smaller and naturally there was always a scrambling for this portion.

One hundred and twenty men were supposed to cook on it. That meant about fifteen different messes were to cook their meal during the main evening meal. The messes cooked at once, one from each end of the block and they were allowed thirty minutes, no longer! So the time for the evening meal usually took about four hours. To make it possible for each mess to eat at a fair time, a rotation system was worked out whereby each day your mess went on the stove a half hour earlier. The reason for using the stove for only one meal was the scarcity of fuel. Again, Kriegie ingenuity came to the fore and little one-pot stoves began to crop up in various parts of the building where a connection could be made with the old chimneys. These little stoves were usually about one square foot and were made of brick and clay and the chimney of tin cans. This helped to alleviate much of the congestion on the main stove and also at least gave us a hot drink for the other two meals. A little fire pit was useful for roasting potatoes. We were allowed about one small bucket of coal bricketts per eight men per day and part of this became our share to the big stove to keep it going. Obviously, this was also a focal point of heat in the building, in fact, it was the only source of heat. This made it an advantage to have your mess located near the stove, for warmth, but a decided disadvantage was the terrible congestion around it at all times."

From the Geneva Convention relative to the treatment of prisoners of war: Food rations must be sufficient in quality, quantity and variety to keep PWs in good health and avoid loss of weight or nutritional deficencies.

ALLIED CAMP LEADERS

THE SENIOR RANKING OFFICER was normally, ex officio, the prisoner's leader in the Oflags and officer's compounds of the Stalags. NCO airmen, however, took less cognisance of rank and elected their own leaders by democratic vote.

On 9th August 1941, Wing Commander Douglas Bader led a wing of fighters out of Tangmere on a bomber escort mission. Over St. Omer, the Spitfires tangled with a Luftwaffe Geschwader. In the combat, Bader's plane was sliced in two by the prop of a diving Messerschmitt, and one of his artificial legs stayed in the cockpit when he baled out. A spare was dropped by the crew of an RAF Blenheim, escorted by Spitfires, but the Germans had already retrieved, repaired and restored the original limb to the Wing Commander as he lay in hospital. Thus equipped, and aided by a brave young maid, he climbed out of a window and took refuge in the home of a peasant couple on the outskirts of the town. Another female worker at the hospital, less favourably disposed toward Bader, betrayed his escape plan and he was soon recaptured. He was incarcerated in several prison camps, the last of which was Colditz Castle, where he remained, with other prominent escapees, until the war was won.

When he became Senior Allied Officer of the Centre Compound, Sagan, Col. Delmar Spivey met the problem of camp organization and administration head-on: "We set out at once to organize the camp into a military unit. All of the Americans were called together and told of the plan. It was explained that each of us was still in the Army and liable to the Articles of War even though not directly under military control. I assured the American POWs that I had the authority and would invoke the Articles if necessary. A promise from the Kommandant had assured me that he intended to let us run the camp with the least possible interference from him and that he, under the Geneva Convention, would hold me responsible for the conduct of the camp. This gave me courage and hope that we could improve our lot.

"The reaction to this meeting as a whole was not good. The British merely chuckled. Advocates of the Iron Fist type of control believed that the only way to get the Americans to band together for their own good was to be positive and ruthless. Those of us who were older and more experienced in dealing with men realized this was no place or time for harsh and unreasonable measures. The appearance in camp of two of my closest and most able friends, Colonel Bill Kennedy and Danny Jenkins, bolstered the experience and ability of the Center Compound staff to the point where it was, in my opinion, as good as that of any air force unit existing anywhere in the world at that time. It made me sad to see these friends as POWs, but it was a blessing for all of us in Center Compound. We held fast to our decision to run the camp in a military manner, giving orders and demanding that they be carried out. Our approach was not just firm but geared to an understanding of the situation. We determined to lead, guide, direct, and encourage instead of being arbitrary. I do not know what I would have done if the group had steadfastly refused to cooperate. At the moment I was too busy to worry about whether they would do so or not, but they did.

"One of the first things on the program was a general clean-up of the compound and a gradual improvement in personal hygiene and appearance. I have been told that when either men or women have to live by themselves, free of the customs imposed by organized society, they revert to animal instinct insofar as cleanliness and orderliness are concerned. Without doubt this was true of a majority of the men in Center Compound.

"The lack of proper bathing facilities, soap, changes of clothing, shaving and hair-cutting equipment, the deplorable condition of the barracks, and a general feeling of futility caused this attitude. For the new arrivals, there was the letdown from the terrific strain of battle, accompanied by the desire to shut one's mind to everything until it was possible to escape or until the war ended.

"In order to fight the slovenliness which shocked me so on arrival, a campaign was begun, without fanfare and without orders or antagonisms, to have the men clean themselves up. I was blessed by having men like Red Rawlinson, Charlie Grooms, Sam Magee and several others of their caliber to serve as my barracks or squadron commanders. These men, by their personality, leadership, and forcefulness, accomplished what was necessary without the men in their barracks realizing what was happening.

The process worked beautifully; by the spring of 1944 I was actually proud of the men and their surroundings. Our Saturday morning inspections would have done credit to a first-class military unit back in the United States. However, not all the men were willing to do their part.

Many believed the authority of the SAO was fictitious and could not be enforced. Some believed they owed no allegiance to the will of the camp as a whole, nor did they care to consider what inconvenience the camp suffered as a result of their individualistic actions.

They maintained that their instructions to escape were the only ones they intended to obey. Much of this lack of discipline can be traced to the faulty briefings on escape by inexperienced intelligence officers who developed and expounded theories of their own. The mavericks in our otherwise disciplined herd had to be dealt with individually. If the barracks commander couldn't take care of the situation, the man was brought to me; if I couldn't reason with him he became the ward of the strong-arm squad of his barracks. This squad was organized for and trained in commando tactics in case a situation ever developed where we had to fight for our lives. They weren't averse to manhandling a lad who wouldn't obey camp orders, nor were they beyond taking a camp inmate who wouldn't bathe to the ice-cold shower and scrubbing him with a GI brush and Octagon soap. These cases were few. As a general rule I could rely on the men carrying out any order given them. I never ordered a man scrubbed!"

When Hub Zemke arrived at Stalag Luft I, Barth, he was the highest-ranking Allied officer and found himself in charge of POWs at one of the largest German prison camps for British, U.S., and other Allied airmen. Faced with a slowly starving camp, brutal weather conditions on the Baltic coast, and an arrogant and oppressive Luftwaffe administration, Zemke's priority became the survival of every POW in his command. "Unlike my previous military appointments, this one offered no shortage of time to meditate upon the problems of command. During those first days at Barth I thought hard and long about the situation. The Senior Allied Officer could be no more than a figurehead and mouthpiece for the POW organization, but that was not to my satisfaction. It was reasoned that the overriding aim must be the welfare of the prisoners. And I had to see that when the day of liberation came all, or as many as possible, were still alive and well. Despite the new Wehrmacht offensive in the west, the Third Reich would surely crumble before next summer. There was frequent speculation in the camp as to what would happen in the last throes of the Nazi regime. Some thought the Germans would exterminate us as a last act of spite. I did not consider this a serious possibility but did expect the Allied POWs to be used as hostages in some attempt to bargain. Whatever happened, our best chance of survival lay in our own preparedness for any eventuality. Thus it was my objective to strengthen the POW organization by every means available and at the same time to get the German camp administration to recognize it as an efficient setup to be reckoned with.

"I had already been amazed by many of the enterprises being successfully pursued in the camp, largely unknown to our captors. The ability to tackle just about anything was not so surprising when one considered that we had more than 5,000 men drawn from all walks of life and all trades and professions. This abundance of talents, though handicapped by the serious restraints of confinement as it was, should still have been able to outwit the Luftwaffe staff and the sulking guards. While they attempted to subjugate and condition us to accepting our servitude, we had to strive to keep them under pressure at every opportunity to sustain our own morale and crack theirs. Such objectives were undoubtedly those of my predecessors, which I now intended to pursue with the same determination. It was only natural that the old hands would resent any interference from this upstart newcomer, a situation to which I was sensitive. Time should bring acceptance, and for now it would be prudent not to interfere with established procedures.

"While it was vital that our keepers should be encouraged to see the prisoners as a well-organized and disciplined body of men rather than as a helpless collection of humanity, we also had to work on those Germans who were either sympathetic to us and disillusioned with their own masters or just plain corruptible. This aim, of course, had been pursued with vigor long before I arrived on the scene. As Senior Allied Officer I saw my part in the scheme of things as one of sizing up the senior German administrators and working on those who showed signs of sympathy.

" The German camp administration pinned up a bulletin daily in each compound at Barth, giving their version of the war news. The prisoners had for some time, been countering the German's propaganda sheet with a daily news bulletin of their own, an innocuous publication published with German approval, containing news culled from German newspapers and radio broadcasts, and information gathered from new arrivals in the camp. A copy was distributed to each barracks and a designated reader read it to all who were interested. One unintended function served by this paper was that it helped give cover to another, and secret, daily news sheet."

Twice a day, news broadcasts from the BBC were monitored—on secret radios—by certain prisoners in the West compound, who wrote down the news information in long hand and passed it to the West compound security officer, who concealed the papers in a Klim tin that had been fitted with a false bottom. The next morning, after the appell, if there were no barracks searches by the Germans, he dictated the 'news' information to a typist who then handed the typed copy to an official liaison officer who had to get permission of the camp authorities to make a daily trip carrying messages and papers between the Senior British Officer in West compound and Col. Zemke, SAO in North I. This liaison officer smuggled the copy in his wristwatch case, from which the works had been removed. The hands of the watch, however, could still be adjusted to show the correct time of day when he passed the compound guards for inspection. He then entered the barracks of the SAO, North I, and read the news to 1st Lt. D. MacDonald, after which he immediately burned the copy he had carried.

MacDonald then prepared four copies of an 'Americanized' version of the news, one for each of the North compounds and the U.S. contingent in the West compound, and this was then called the POW-WOW. Each copy of the POW-WOW was taken to the barracks' security officers who then arranged for the regular reader of the 'approved' camp news bulletin to also read the secret news from the BBC to the men at their noon meal. The POW-WOW was read first, as it was of greater interest to the audience, and if the Germans were to unexpectedly arrive, the reader would quickly switch to reading the camp news bulletin. After the reading, all copies of the POW-WOW were consumed in the stoves leaving no evidence of their existence.

Colonel Zemke: "I had no idea where the radio was hidden or that there were two. The first had been constructed by two RAF men, mainly from smuggled parts, soon after Stalag Luft I became 'officers-only' late in 1943. At first operated on the camp electrical system, it was converted to run on flashlight batteries in order to listen to the BBC night broadcast when the camp electricity supply had been cut off. The receiver was concealed within a wall panel located behind a bed in the barracks room, some of the fixing nails acting as terminals to which an aerial wire and earphone cable could be attached. A second radio, a German civilian set, was obtained by a British Army private working in North compound as an orderly, but whose undercover task was to 'encourage' a particular German to talk. When received, the set was found to be faulty, and as North compound could not get it to function it was smuggled in to the West compound inside a large soap box for the RAF radio experts to work on. When eventually brought into operation, this set was hidden in the camp theater behind a false cupboard back.

"It was permissible for next of kin to send clothing, sports items and games, books, cigarettes, tobacco, and food. These would periodically arrive in large consignments at the Barth railroad station. A truck was sent to collect them with a small party of POWs to do the loading under guard. The building that served as the parcel store was in the Vorlager, where the parcels were brought and censored. A team of POWs were assembled in the parcel store to sort packages for the different compounds and then to open each for examination by the German censors. Any food cans were always punctured at one end to ensure the contents would be quickly consumed and not kept for escape purposes. Cigarette and tobacco packets were exposed but only occasionally did a censor examine one. All books were taken away and, if approved, later issued to the POW library. Games and clothing parcels were untied by the prisoners before being passed along a table for the censor's examination, after which they were retied and put in sacks for distribution.

"Coded messages in letters told us well in advance the names of the individuals to whom forbidden material was being sent, and the POW sorters were briefed on these. An aid to identification was that the packages containing the secret enclosures were always postmarked Alabama. When a sorter saw an Alabama postmark he alerted other POW sorters to distract the censor's attention while the special parcel was diverted to a sack of already censored parcels.

"Some of the material sent was so cleverly and securely concealed that it was allowed to pass before the German censors without prior interception. Double-skin tins were a common method of getting maps, money, film, and thin items to us. Hollow spools of thread, the handles of table tennis paddles, and like objects contained the more bulky contraband such as radio tubes and camera parts.

"The sleight of hand of a conjurer was developed by some of the sorters in diverting the parcels they recognized as containing forbidden items. If any had been apprehended the punishment would have been severe.

"The censoring of mail both into and out of the camp was done by German interpreters at Stalag Luft III, Sagan. Coded messages were suspected and anything that looked ambiguous was blacked out—or anything not understood was regarded as suspicious. They also checked for the use of invisible ink. As far as is known they never discovered any of the many forms of coded messages that passed between POWs and the British and American agencies involved. In case they should be shot down and made prisoner, selected members of Allied air crews were taught codes to be used in correspondence with next of kin. When any of these men were notified as POWs, their letters home were intercepted and decoded. Letters containing coded messages were drafted by the intelligence people in the States and Britain to send to these POWs, who passed the information to compound security officers. The messages sent from the camp were mostly concerned with intelligence obtained from new POWs that was believed to be important in aiding the Allied cause.

"Successfully hiding forbidden articles and material from our captors was always difficult and again there were some ingenious solutions. A considerable library of books had been built up over the months for POW use and it was within the covers and bindings of selected volumes that forged documents, German bank notes, maps, etc. were concealed. Only a very few people knew of this and the majority of POW readers enjoyed these books without knowing the secrets they held."

From the Geneva Convention relative to the treatment of prisoners of war: Articles 73. In power of enemy power; treated with humanity; reprisals prohibited—Prisoners of war are in the power of the enemy power, but not of the individuals or bodies of troops who capture them. They must at all times be treated with humanity and protected, particularly against acts of violence, insults, and public curiosity. Measures of reprisal against them are prohibited. 78-81 concern the important matters of requests and complaints as to the conditions of detention, of relations between PWs and the authorities, and of the appointment of prisoners' representatives who must be allowed ready access to the representatives of the protecting power.

FUN AND GAMES

THIS IS WHAT ROBERT KEE remembered about the way that the Kriegies passed the long and slow hours of Stalag life: "For the bureaucratic minded there was camp administration, and there were good and bad bureaucrats. For readers there were books and rooms set apart as libraries, and there were people who learnt a great deal and people who read furiously and learnt nothing. For actors and producers and carpenters there was a theatre and for people who liked seeing plays there was an auditorium. For those who liked cleaning their buttons there was button polish and a British parade once a year on the King's birthday. For those who 'liked a job to do' there was the distribution of food and clothing and fuel, and there were some who did it honestly and others who were suspected of turning it into a 'racket'. For those who liked to go to church there were padres of several denominations and candles and a camp-built altar. And there were class rooms and classes where nobody learnt very much but everybody thought they were doing something. Games players cleared areas of sand or dusty rubble. Strategists pinned up maps. Gardeners dug gardens. And people who liked to walk and talk walked round and round the perimeter track in endless identical circles."

Certainly, the Anglo-Saxon dedication to ball-games found several outlets at Sagan. The sand-covered parade ground provided a football pitch (with penalties for kicking the ball over the fence), a concrete strip was available for cricket, and a limited variety of golf was played on a nine-hole pitch-and-putt course with home-made clubs and balls. After D-Day, when the SBO decided that the prisoners must attain a state of fitness for whatever was to come, training began for a relay race around the 900 yard circuit between teams of fifty from each of the eight blocks. With the race still some weeks away, it was not uncommon for 400 men to be jogging, running or sprinting, and passing batons hand to hand. "One expert in athletics," Bobby Stark wrote, "remarked that many national teams had gone into the Olympics with less preparation." The race began shortly after 2:30 in the afternoon, and the winning block's last runner broke the tape at 5:15. The day was very hot, and many a competitor ran on into the fire pool..

In the prisoners' huts, the hours passed slowly in the winter evenings. The low voltage of the light bulbs made reading difficult, and men occupied themselves with all sorts of card games, with chess and even with such child's games as snakes and ladders, tiddly-winks and ludo.

Outdoor sports sometimes provided cover for escape activities. In the famous "Trojan Horse" escape from Sagan, for example, the entrance to the tunnel lay beneath a vaulting horse, in which the diggers were carried to and fro, and the trapdoor to another was concealed beneath a rugby scrum when an exhausted digger had to be brought up. "The Germans knew very little about rugby football," Halifax navigator Stark explained. "We enlarged the scrum to twelve or more each side, and as scrum-half I kept putting the ball in until the referee was finally satisfied it was put in straight."

"We had rats," said Don Ackerson, "one of which was so big and strong that he was seen going off with a whole piece of German bread, a 'Superrat' feat. After lights out we amused ourselves by lighting farts which can be seen to burn with a clear blue flame.

Outside, the guards patrolled with dogs. We could see the rockets going up from the rocket site at Peenemunde about 50 miles to the east. At that time we didn't know what these vertical vapor trails were. We also amused ourselves by waving at the pilot who towed the target sleeve for the local flak school. He flew low over the camp as he came back to the airfield. This fun came to an end when a bunch of the guys threw rocks at him when he came over low one day. That was the end. We also had fun when a British RAF Mosquito came over and shot up the airfield one day. A Fw-190 took off and got on his tail. Just at the last moment, another Mosquito came out of the clouds and shot the Fw-190 down. We all cheered like mad which made the guards mad as hell. We cheered every time the 8th Air Force came over. Finally, we had to go in the barracks as soon as the air raid siren blew. Later still, we had the shutters locked at night, which was a real pain. The only fun then was rattling the shutters when the guard dog came around. The dog would go mad trying to get to us through the wooden shutters. We also had fun when Max Schmelling was brought to the camp to build good will. Some idiots asked for his autograph. All of us got his picture so we could line all the urinals with them and the whole camp then took great delight in visiting the latrines."

Burt Joseph of the 100th Bomb Group, US Eighth Air Force, whose burning B-17 went down over Braunschweig, was Kriegie No. 1843 to the enemy authorities, but to his messmates at Stalag Luft III, at least initially, he was 'Bitter Joe'—on account of his unconcealed displeasure at being clobbered on his last combat mission. Gradually, however, he began to make the most of what Sagan had to offer. "Weather permitting," he remembered, "we engaged in various sports, such as touch football. We had an All-American football player from the University of Minnesota who refused to play because he was afraid of being injured, and [then] be unable to play professional ball when the war was over."

Joseph also found some humour in the daily German round: "Announcements by the camp staff to the inmates were made at appell, when we were counted twice each day. Our response to many of these was 'Hubba, Hubba'. Occasionally, this irritated the staff officers and they would shout 'Vas ist mit der Hubba, Hubba'?"

From the Geneva Convention relative to the treatment of prisoners of war: Articles 34-38 guarantee PWs enjoyment of religious, intellectual, and physical activities, and require facilities to be furnished for out-of-doors exercise.

RED CROSS PARCELS

AS 1943 DREW TO AN END, Wing Commander Leonard Cheshire, the famous leader of No. 617 Squadron, conceived a plan to brighten Christmas Day for the inmates of Stalag Luft III, among whom, it so happened, was his brother Chris. Cheshire proposed that he and two of his most experienced pilots (the Australian Dam Busters 'Mickey' Martin and David Shannon), should fly a daylight mission to Sagan at low level, each with a bomb bay full of foodstuffs and goodies to drop inside the wire. The scheme was vetoed at high level, on the grounds that the camp guards might suspect an arms-drop and mow the prisoners down as they ran to fetch the parcels. Cheshire was crestfallen, but Martin and Shannon, brave men as they were, were somewhat relieved.

"Hail, hail Red Cross!" wrote Frank Kautzmann on 7th March 1945, "I knew you would come through for us. Today, I enjoyed a delicious breakfast of toasted German bread tidbits that tasted just like Grapenuts. With a little sprinkled sugar and the last of our Klim milk we managed to turn it into a breakfast that reminded us of home. In addition, we enjoyed two thin slices of bread with our Kriegie cheese spread on one and prune margarine on the other."

"If it weren't for the Red Cross," he continued the next day, "we'd all die. I've made myself a promise that when I get home, I will do my best to support the Red Cross."

Radio-gunner Roger Armstrong, of the 91st Bomb Group stationed at Bassingbourn, spent the bulk of his POW time at Stalag Luft IV: "We received one No.10 Red Cross Food parcel a week when I arrived at Stalag Luft IV. This ration was suddenly cut to one half parcel a week, and later to a quarter parcel, after Christmas. It usually contained about the same items but occasionally there was some variation. The following was what could be found, at times, in the cardboard food parcel: Corned beef or C rations-12 oz., Canned Spam-12 oz., Butter-16 oz., Cheese-8 oz., Paté-6 oz., Peanut butter-8 oz., D-Bars (chocolate)(2)-8 oz., Tuna, salmon or sardines-8 oz., salt and pepper, Prunes or raisins-8 oz., Milk (powdered)-16 oz., Coffee (soluable)-4 oz., Sugar (cubes)-8 oz., Cigarettes-4 to 5 packs, Jam-6 oz., Soap-2 bars, Vitamin C pills-7 day supply.

"During my six and a half months stay at Stalag Luft IV and Luft I, on rare occasions we received the following German garrison foods: Barley cereal, dried pea soup, potatoes with Argentine corned beef, rogan soup mix, carrots, turnips, German jam, sugar, ersatz coffee, dehydrated (cabbage, carrots, seaweed) and cheese. These were very small portions .

"On Christmas day the Germans allowed a special Red Cross package, made up in the U.S., to be issued each American. In addition, the British Red Cross sent a special Christmas package to each of their men. There was a surplus, so the Germans allowed the Americans to share in one quarter of a British parcel. The British parcel had the traditional English food for Christmas, so I had a small portion of Plum Pudding. In addition, the Germans gave each room two buckets of hot boiled beans. They tasted so good, most of us threw up but still ate more boiled beans. By now my stomach had shrunk and it was just too much of a good thing.

"The special American Red Cross parcel contained: one 12 oz. can of turkey, a 16 oz. can of plum pudding, a 4 oz. can of Vienna sausages, a 6 oz. can of whole cherries, a 4 oz. can of preserved butter, a 4 oz. can of deviled ham, a 6 oz. can of honey, a 6 oz. can of pineapple jam, two 2 oz. fruit bars, a 7 oz. can of mixed nuts, an 8 oz. can of mixed candy, an 8 oz. box of dried dates, 12 bullion cubes, 3 packs of chewing gum, 3 packs of cigarettes, a pipe, 1 package of pipe tobacco, 1 wash cloth, 1 deck of playing cards, 1 deck of Michigan Rummy, and one colored 8 x 10 photo of an American scene. It became an unforgettable Christmas. Each Christmas, I think back to the Christmas of 1944."

Hubert 'Hub' Zemke, commanding officer of the 56th and 479th Fighter Groups, 8 USAAF, and Senior Allied Officer at Stalag Luft I, recalled: "My own experience during just a few weeks of captivity had demonstrated how a lack of food and warmth can have a dampening effect upon the morale of the individual. While the Germans certainly had their problems with food at this stage in the war, the only thing to be said for that supplied to Stalag Luft I POWs was that it kept men from starving. Without doubt hunger was intentionally induced with the aim of subduing the internees. The German food was prepared in a central kitchen by the POW volunteers and distributed to the compounds once a day. For the most part it consisted of vegetables—potatoes, turnips, and various sorts of beet and cabbage. Occasionally there would be a small piece of horsemeat. A thin barley soup and black bread were fairly regular features of the menu. Fortunately there were Red Cross food parcels to supplement the German rations, each prisoner normally being issued one per week. Every parcel had about a dozen different foodstuffs in cans or packs plus soap and cigarettes. The canned meats, sardines, jams, and candies provided the necessary extra nourishment for our diet, as well as giving amateur cooks the opportunity to try and make the prison rations more palatable.

"The Red Cross also provided blankets and uniform clothing, although such was the influx of new prisoners during the summer and fall of 1944 that there was now a shortage."

As for next-of-kin parcels, the British Red Cross War Organisation Official History 1939-1945 states:

Article 11 of the Geneva Convention of 1929 reads: "The food ration of prisoners of war shall be equivalent in quantity and quality to that of the depot troops . . ." Diet differs considerably between peoples, even for example, between British, German and Italian peoples. To a much greater degree does the difference exist between the British and Japanese peoples. The food ration prescribed by the Convention would be one to which the prisoners were unaccustomed. Apart from any question of quality or quantity, their health during a long period of captivity would be likely to suffer if they were restricted to the food provided for the depot troops of the Detaining Power. Hence provision in the Convention for prisoners to receive supplementary food.

Article 37 authorises prisoners to receive individually postal parcels containing foodstuffs and other articles intended for consumption or clothing. The British Government (and other Governments) attached conditions to this facility. The British Government limited the number of parcels which could be sent to a prisoner to one every three months. It also prohibited the inclusion of food in the parcels, as it had made the Prisoners of War Department of the War Organisation the accredited authority for providing supplementary food supplies to the prisoners.

Food was not allowed because the War Organisation was itself providing a regular service of food parcels. There were, of course, other reasons—keeping qualities, difficulties of satisfactory packing with other articles, and suitability for prisoners' needs. Medical comforts were also adequately supplied by the Invalid Comforts Section of the War Organisation. Books and music, tobacco and cigarettes, were also provided by the War Organisation, and the public were able, in addition, to send these articles through the "permit" system.

As the service became stabilised, a list of prohibited articles could be drawn up for circulation to next-of-kin. From time to time, it was altered, but the changes were not substantial. In June 1944, the list included:

Food—except solid chocolate

Written communications (all letters to prisoners of war must be sent by letter post).

Books, note books, music or any printed matter.

Pictorial illustrations and photographs.

Money, stamps, stationery and playing cards.

Articles in glass containers, tubes, tins and other receptacles which are breakable or cannot easily be opened for inspection.

Badges of Regiments formed since September 3rd, 1939, and all formations. These include Commandos, Paratroops and Airborne Units, R.E.M.E., etc.

Candles, spirits or solidified spirit for cooking stoves, matches or any other inflammable material. Complete suits, coloured or grey flannel trousers, black and dark coloured shirts, civilian ties, sports coats or blazers, mackintoshes, windcheaters, leather waistcoats or any kind of civilian overcoat. (These, excepting black shirts, may, however, be sent to civilian internees).

Fountain pens and pen nibs.

Glass mirrors.

Gum boots, Wellingtons and goloshes.

Haversacks.

Medical comforts. This includes medicines of all kinds, drugs, pills, pastilles and bandages.

Nail files.

Photographic apparatus, field glasses, sextants, compasses, electric torches and other instruments that could be used for Naval and Military purposes.

Rubber soles and heels.

Sleeping bags (padded), cushions or pillows.
Sleeping suits other than pyjamas.
Soap flakes and soap powders.
Tobacco, cigarettes.
Toilet paper.
Watches, scissors (except small nail scissors), knives and tools.

The weight of the parcel, including such additions of chocolate and soap as next-of-kin wished the Packing Centre to add, was not permitted to exceed 10 lbs. The rule about chocolate was strict: only solid chocolate was allowed. Chocolate with any kind of filling was prohibited. Much was wasted, because next-of-kin paid no attention to this instruction, and quantities of sweets had also to be removed from the POW parcels, as all were banned. Indeed, notwithstanding efforts to make known the prohibited and permitted articles, the examiners found many of the former which had to be returned to the senders.

To next-of-kin the composition of a parcel was a serious business. When goods became scarce in the shops, suitable articles were more difficult to find. The purchase tax, also, if goods were bought in this way, increased the outlay. Coupons gave rise to further difficulty. To build up a parcel a prisoner would wish to receive and to obtain the best value for the expenditure was a problem upon which many next-of-kin required and welcomed guidance and advice. To some, regimental associations offered practical help. For others, local prisoners of war committees were at hand. Joint county committees of the War Organisation set up a network of packing centres throughout the country. The Prisoners of War Department supplied them with lists of prisoners whose home addresses were in their respective counties. The Central Hospital Supply Service formed special work parties to produce articles for next-of-kin parcels. At the beginning of 1944, in England and Wales, 157 local packing centres of the joint county committees and the Central Hospital Service Supply were in operation. To the, to complete the picture, there are to be added the regimental associations and other bodies engaged on the same service.

The help which they were able to give to next-of-kin was considerable. They saw to it that prohibited articles were not included in the parcels. And they securely packed the parcels for dispatch to the central packing centres. They made sure that all the lists and labels were correctly set out.

General Albert P. Clark provided the text of this letter written to him at Stalag Luft III, by his father, a doctor, in April 1943:

Dear Bub,

Your fine letter written February 5 arrived on Ruth's birthday. It had a hole in it as big as your thumb but we supplied all the words. Don't worry about the Red Cross packages and nutrition, I have you covered if Carolyn's packages ever get there; you will have plenty of vitamins and minerals in each to outlast the period between. First one left on December 18 to December 25, and every sixty days thereafter. The tablets are to be taken 1-3 times a day, but if you have a little reserve you might well take one extra one a day.

I have also sent powdered egg and powdered milk. Most of the other things are forbidden, we are sorry to say—even books. I try to make each letter a little lecture on survival. The symptoms of even a slight lack of vitamins or minerals, or certain nitrogen foods, are so hard to see and find in the early stages that even most physicians can't diagnose them. One of the first is swollen, puffy gums near the edge or surface of the tooth—gums that bleed easily—due to lack of vitamin C (civitamic or ascorbic acid) which you get from citrus or tomatoes, or vegetables, potatoes, greens, cabbage—all preferably raw.

Fight flies at source—they breed in warm, moist, contaminated spots and look like tiny white or gray worms (maggots). They take the color of the wet muck in which they develop from eggs you can't see. It takes seven to ten days from egg to fly. Keep flies out of warm, moist places by killing all adults. Keep them from hatching by burning the warm, moist places if you can't dry them up. Build fly traps and bait them with scraps of wet, smelly food. Flies can't stand being dried. Fly larvae can't stand heat. Wood and coal ashes contain lye and kill flies while breeding. Wood and coal ashes if mixed with water and allowed to settle gives you a lye solution with which you can scrub, clean, and even make soap by mixing it with any fat. Just boil the solution from ashes until concentrated, and when still warm stir in the strained fat that has been melted. If it stings the hands add a little more fat and warm again, and stir well once more. If it feels greasy, add a little more settled ash water and warm, and stir again. Put aside to dry. The pioneers had no other soap. If you have plenty of settled, concentrated ash water, pour it into latrines by sprinkling, to kill flies as a substitute for lime.

If each man in your outfit can find himself an old nail, iron or steel, and remove rust, then with a stone, file off a little iron filings every day or so and put it on the tongue and wash it down with water—the stomach will change it to iron chloride. This will keep up their iron reserve and prevent anemia. Your pictures show you warmly clad, and I can see your watch and class ring. You look in good health, but don't assume you are or will continue to be, unless you take special precautions and use every bit of health and nutritional knowledge I have been able to give you in the past, or can give you in the future.

Get every minute of sunlight you can on as much of the body as possible. Exercise enough to keep your muscles hard and your circulation in good shape, but not enough to burn up too much food, and fat especially. Kill rats and burn bodies to reduce fleas and lice from them. Inspect for bedbugs and clean them out. Little black spots in a short chain on pillow cases, or sheets if you have them, or on sleeping clothes indicate bedbugs. Coal oil, gasoline, or even strong lye water will kill them and eggs. Fight mosquitoes if present. Eliminate water in any standing puddles or tin cans, or eave troughs, or catch basins or unused water traps. Sleep every man head to foot to avoid his secretions in the air.

Can you build any kind of bomb shelter, such as shallow prone trenches? Try to write me what you eat in detail for a day or a week and let me evaluate your nutrition, and tell me how much physical work you do in a day, and let me evaluate your needs. How much salt can you get? Is it iodized, if you know? Do you get any fish or seafood?

Our garden is growing. My job grows heavier. Carolyn received your letter of January 16 and I read it. We all join in love—Dad.
note: Organize massage classes which will not burn up too much carbohydrate and leach out of you too much vitamin B-1, and yet will keep your circulation and muscles in shape.

From the Geneva Convention relative to the treatment of prisoners of war: It is provided in Article 69 that the PW shall be permitted to send out a 'capture card' addressed to the 'Central Prisoners of War Agency' for its card index system. Article 71 concerns PW correspondence and entitles them to mail a minimum of 2 letters and 4 cards each month. This minimum may be reduced if the protecting power finds that to be required by necessary censorship. PWs are also allowed to send telegrams under certain circumstances. The right of prisoners' representatives to take possession of collective relief shipments and to distribute them, as desired by donors, is recognized in Article 73. Such relief shipments are exempt from import, customs and other dues (Article 74). Where military operations prevent compliance with the Convention's requirements as to transport of these shipments, such transport may be undertaken by the International Red Cross (Article 75).

CAMP COMMANDANT

IT WAS EARLY IN SEPTEMBER 1940 when Douglas Connolly, the Irish wireless operator who was shot down over Bremerhaven, arrived at Stalag Luft I, Barth, north-east of Rostock on the Baltic coast of Pomerania. "The Commandant was an Austrian," said Connolly. "He told us he didn't like Germans, and he couldn't do enough for us. He gave us a common room, with a loud-speaker installed, and let us listen to the BBC news last thing at night. We used the common room for planning escapes—what we didn't know was that it was bugged. Every time a tunnel got too near the wire, the Commandant arrived with his merry men and dismantled it. But he was really a heck of a nice feller . . ."

Colonel Delmar T. Spivey entered Stalag Luft III in late July 1943. He was twice the age of most of his fellow inmates, and his seniority and West Point training positioned him as the new Allied camp leader. Within two weeks, Spivey assumed command of the Center Compound, Sagan, as SOA, Senior Allied Officer. "One of the first things I did when I got into Center Compound was to request an interview with the camp Kommandant, Oberst von Lindeiner. He received me as graciously as if I were one of his own most senior staff members. He stood up behind his desk, very tall and erect, and remained standing until I was seated. Never once during the entire time he was Kommandant did he fail to treat me with respect traditionally shown to a colonel in the Army. He spoke English and was definitely an officer of the old school, well educated, Prussian in looks and manner. He admitted to being a Nazi, but I do not believe he was a very devout one. I always felt he would do his duty toward us. This was reassuring.

"Through my first and subsequent interviews I learned what Kommandant von Lindeiner expected of us and what his attitude toward us would be. He told me that the Reich had placed all POWs under the O.K.W. (Ober Kommandoder Wehrmacht) and that as Air Force POWs we were directly under the German Luftwaffe. The Gestapo, which acted independently of all other authority, was not involved in camp administration but did deal with escapes and subversive activities and was dreaded by Germans and POWs alike. All of us who knew the Oberst felt that

he would have done much more for us had it not been for this
terrible organization which could cause a man to disappear forever.
The Kommandant gave me much advice which proved helpful
later on. He told me how difficult it would be for me to
understand how the Germans thought and acted, their love of
regimentation and orderliness; and their inability to comprehend
American humor and attitudes toward life in general and toward
military life in particular. He promised us many things which he
was never able to bring about because of restrictions and fear of
the Gestapo. His deputy, Major Gustav Simoleit, was a college
professor who spoke five languages fluently and had a professor's
approach to everything. Simoleit remained with the camp until
liberation and eased many a Kriegie's pain without the POW's
knowledge."

According to the rules, Lt. Col. von Lindeiner, the Commandant at
Sagan, should have used the German language, and the services of
an interpreter, in his dealings with the prisoners. This was one of
the many rules he constantly ignored, and it was given in evidence
against him at his subsequent court martial that, at all his weekly
meetings with the senior British and Americans, he had invariably
greeted them with handshakes and spoken with them in English.
Furthermore, on three occasions, he had sent birthday greetings
to senior prisoners and provided them with wine. He had failed
to realize, ran the indictment, that his approaches would only be
regarded as weakness, and above all, "he forgot the misery and
suffering that the 'terror airmen' had brought to German men and
cities, and that no good German should shake hands with such
enemies and give them presents."

In his introduction to The Memoirs of Colonel Friedrich-Wilhelm
von Lindeiner-Wildau, Kommandant, Stalag Luft III, Arthur Durand
said of him: "He was a proud and capable businessman and
officer from the old school of German soldiers. When von
Lindeiner assumed command of the camp, he was sixty-one
years old, had a distinguished military career with two Iron
Crosses to his credit, and had clearly indicated his displeasure
with the recent turn of events in his beloved Germany. Severely
wounded three times in World War I, he was never able to return

to active combat. Most observers have rated von Lindeiner very highly as a camp commander. He was well educated and spokefluent English. One report states that he was a man with whom 'a shouting match was out of the question.' Perhaps the most telling comment on the man came from the former Stalag Luft III prisoner who wrote: 'No Kommandant, to a prisoner, is a good man, but I think von Lindeiner was.' "

The first United States Army Air Force pilot to become Senior Allied Officer at Sagan, was Lt. Col. Albert P. Clark, on 15th August 1942. Of Colonel von Lindeiner he wrote in the preface to von Lindeiner's memoirs: "POWs in the camp at Sagan respected Col. von Lindeiner for his genuine efforts to make life bearable and to abide by the Geneva Accords. The camp was regularly inspected by representatives of the Protecting Power (Switzerland), and we had frequent and uninhibited communication with them. While prisoners of war can never be expected to be satisfied with their lot, the significance of the standards which the Luftwaffe and von Lindeiner sought to maintain can be grasped when one realizes that Russian prisoners were being allowed to die of neglect by the millions and masses of political prisoners were being exterminated elsewhere in Germany.

"In some respects, Colonel von Lindeiner's efforts to improve living conditions in the camp were a matter of self-interest. His theory was that supporting cultural, athletic and educational activities in a clean and relatively livable environment would discourage escape attempts and lessen the danger of a takeover of the camp by the SS or Gestapo, which was a very real and serious threat. Unfortunately, in the officer camps the logic of this view was lost amid the ceaseless and inspired struggle of a high percentage of the prisoners to continue the war by all means—intelligence, blackmail, sabotage and escape. One element of the prisoner psychology involved ridicule of the Germans and everything they did. Thus most of von Lindeiner's efforts went unacknowledged by all except the most responsible of the senior prisoner leadership.

"Von Lindeiner's efforts to prevent his garrison personnel from creating emotional incidents in their daily relationships with the prisoners were a never ending challenge. The prisoners constantly badgered and ridiculed the ferrets and the guards, many of whom were disabled combat veterans or had lost their families and homes in the bombing. It is not surprising that we had a few pot shots ino our crowded camp.

"Colonel von Lindeiner was sacked and court-martialed in late 1944, after the Great Escape. Only the confusion inherent in the collapse of Germany and the intervention of a psychiatrist and friend who consigned him to an asylum to insure his safety prevented his incarceration. Colonel von Lindeiner was then held prisoner by the English for almost two years after the war in spite of his non-involvement in the execution of the fifty RAF escapees from the tunnel at Sagan. By any standards he was shabbily treated, and this is reflected in the bitterness displayed in his account. He was an officer of the old school, and his disgust for Hitler and the Nazi regime is unconcealed. His effort to defend the German armed forces and the Luftwaffe for their honorable treatment of captured allied flyers is understandable."

Colonel von Lindeiner was in command of Stalag Luft III, Sagan, for nearly twenty-two months, from 10th May 1942 until 25th March 1944. The art, science, and activity of escaping was, before, during and after that period, of primary importance to the residents of the camp. In the time of the colonel's command and administration at Sagan, 100 tunnels were constructed or partially constructed, for escape attempts, of which there were 262.

In the parlance of the kriegie, escaping and making it back to one's unit, base or country of origin, was called a 'home run'; the highest possible achievement in baseball and in imprisonment. Planning preparing for, and successfully executing an escape from a camp in a nation unknown to you and that is your enemy, is a hugely demanding and extremely delicate operation. Hundreds, and at times thousands of POWs were involved in such operations, but in all of the colonel's command period, only five escapees made a home run.

As the prisoners gradually became more practiced and experienced in their planning and preparation for escaping, so too did von Lindeiner's personnel become more adept and capable in the area of countermeasures to discover and prevent escape attempts. So efficient were the methods employed at Sagan to combat and foil escapes that the camp was seen as a model in that regard and new POW camp personnel and local criminal police were brought there for specific anti-escape training. Indeed, an 'escape museum' was established for use in that training, and was sited in two barracks filled with escape-related materials that had been located and confiscated in the camp in the period of the colonel's administration.

The prisoner population at Sagan varied, of course, but at the end of von Lindeiner's command in March 1944, it consisted of 6,169 airmen, including 2,581 officers and 408 orderlies of the Royal Air Force and 2,643 officers and 537 orderlies of the United States Army Air Force. By January 1945, the total of inmates had grown to more than 12,000. They had come from the air forces of the United States, Britain, Canada, South Africa, New Zealand, Australia, as well as RAF fliers from Holland, Belgium, Poland, Czechoslovakia, and many volunteers from neutral countries.

Located south of the city of Sagan (now Zagan, Poland) the Stalag Luft III main camp was set up as compounds encompassing an area of slightly less than sixty acres. The compounds were strictly separated and could only be enteres with a special pass. Surrounding each compound was a running double fence three metres high with two metres of separation between the fences. The space was filled with tangled, coiled barbed wire one metre high. Inside the compounds, a line of small stakes ran parallel to and ten metres from the inner fence and a "warning line" wire was affixed to the stakes. Crossing that warning line was expressly forbidden and the guards were authorized to shoot only after giving three warning shouts of 'Halt!'

Outside the compounds, a twenty-foot-high watchtower was located every 75 metres along the fence line. These towers were manned with armed guards day and night. They were issued with a machine-gun, binoculars, and a searchlight to illuminate the fence and compound interior at night. Each tower was in communication with the watch room by telephone. Two guards patrolled outside the fence between the towers at night. To access any compound, a visitor had to first pass through two guarded gates of the front compound.

Escaping attempts through the gates by day or night were difficulte and required the use of excellent disguises and forged papers, skills readily mastered by many of the talented prisoners with ample time to perfect those talents.

With the effectiveness of the German countermeasures, most of the POWs interested in escaping concentrated their efforts on the construction of tunnels, usually from a barracks, under the fencing in into the nearby woods. To counter these efforts, the Germans buried microphones about 100 metres apart at a depth of two metres along the outer fence. The sounds of earth movements registered in a central listening post in the camp.

An open secret was the existence of a POW escape-controlling operation known as "Organization X", responsible for all activity to do with the preparation and execution of escapes, including maintaining the secrecy and security of such activity from discovery by the Germans. It was originally set up and led by Roger Bushell, a South African RAF officer, known as "Big X."

From the beginning of his period of command at Sagan, von Lindeiner made it clear to his prisoner staff officers that he intended the camp to be run along specific guidelines. He told them that the rights and responsibilities of both the German personnel and the prisoners were going to be based on the Geneva Accords of 1929. A kind of "golden rule" premise would operate. He expected his own men to behave towards the prisoners as he would expect the Allies to behave towards him if he were ever so unfortunate as to become their prisoner. He further expected the prisoners to honorably accept their unfortunate situation and to adjust appropriately. At this point one of the British officers interrupted to explain that, while the officer prisoners respected his position, views, and expectations, they wanted to make it clear that it was not only their right but also their duty to try, through successful escape, to rejoin their units at all costs.

The colonel countered that, while he understood that, it was his duty to do all he could to prevent such escapes. The prisoners were, after all, airmen and they should never again be in a position to drop bombs on German territory. They then came to a gentleman's agreement which basically maintained that, while the armed conflict was over for the prisoners, and they were required to accept and adhere to the pertinent international laws and the rules of the camp, they also retained the right and duty to rejoin their units through escaping. Both sides at least appeared to accept that absolute fairness was to be followed in all actions.

The commandant then briefed his own officers, the medical and administrative personnel about what he expected of them in their behaviour towards the prisoners. He said that it was to be based on the Geneva Accords and specifically stated that it was against the tradition of the German soldier to violate the precept of law, humaneness, and chivalry, even against an enemy. He declared that in the last war, there persisted even to the last days—especially between the German Air Force and its enemies—a spirit of chivalry and fellowship, and that their commander-in-chief [Göring] had expressed his wish that in this war also, this spirit should guide the actions of the organizations under him. He told them that, as representatives of the detaining power, they had to view the prisoners as persons who had and still have a duty to fight for their country, as they, the Germans, were doing. He pointed out that the imprisoned enemy is defenceless and to violate his human dignity is contrary to the spirit of chivalry, and that provoking or violent behaviour towards a defenceless people is proof of cowardice. He said it was absolutely essential that all German personnel in the camp were aware of their rights and duties as representatives of the detaining power, and also of the rights and duties of the prisoners. He asked his section commanders to so inform their subordinates.

The commandant ended the briefing by stating that the basis of the behaviour of the German camp personnel was the correct conduct of the prisoners. He said that violations by individual prisoners were to be reported and would be punished, but that the actions of a few should not result in prejudice towards the many. He informed them that it was the right and duty of the prisoner to rejoin his unit by escaping, just as it was the duty of the German personnel to prevent that escape. In conclusion he said, "I ask you not to forget one important fact: any war has an end sooner or later, and after a war the nations have to live together again. We cannot ask for the sympathy of the POW we will release when this war is over, but what we want to instill is a feeling of respect. They can say 'I hate the Germans', but they must think 'I respect them.' "

A kind of honour system evolved which was explained at a meeting of the Allied officers with the camp commandant. The notion of one's word of honour was meant to play an important part of ordinary life in the camp. It had to be given in writing, on a case by case basis, incorporating the signatures of both the prisoner concerned and his senior officer. If affected situations like the issuance of tools. and other items that could potentially be used in escape efforts, and came into play on several occasions in relation to activities such as the construction of the camp auditorium, and other construction projects. The system seemingly worked well. The commandant was at least never aware of any significant violations.

One particular incident occured, however, which von Lindeiner later recalled with some amusement. On the occasion of a visit to the camp by an acquaintance of the colonel, a high-ranking fellow officer, the two men drove in the visitor's car to look at the nearly-completed auditorium being built by the British prisoners. When they arrived at the building site, several British officers came over to see the visitor's car, a model not familiar to them. Well aware of the ability of his prisoners to pilfer items of interest to them, the commandant made sure that the doors and windows of his visitor's car were secure before leaving it to enter the building. Moments later, the visitor's chaufer rushed in to report that a book had somehow been stolen from the locked car.

Colonel von Lindeiner summoned the acting senior Allied officer of the compound and explained to him that the disappearance of the book from the visitor's car was a violation of the honour system gentleman's agreement. He demanded the return of the missing book within two hours. Before that time limit expired the book was safely returned to its owner. However, it now contained two new stamped entries: 'Passed by the British Censor' and 'Seen by Winston Churchill.'

A curious working relationship existed between Colonel von Lindeiner and a man he saw as the most important British officer in the camp, Group Captain Herbert M. Massey. According to the colonel, Group Captain Massey regarded himself as overall Allied leader in the camp and, as a great many American airmen prisoners began arriving, he objected to the U.S. fliers being segregated into their own compound.

Massey was impaired by the effects of a leg wound he had incurred in a 1933 conflict and could walk only with great difficulty. The colonel and Massey respected and trusted each other and, when the German's Berlin apartment was destroyed in a March

1943 RAF bombing raid, Massey and some of the British officers expressed regret over the colonel's loss, adding that they hoped he would never suffer harm at the hands of the RAF. In their working relationship, Massey often asked von Lindeiner for help and support in maintaining his authority among the POWs who would not obey the Group Captain's orders, but the colonel could not give it.

One favour von Lindeiner did do for Massey occurred in the summer of 1943. A prominent English surgeon came to the hospital of a prison camp in central Germany to operate on some seriously wounded British prisoners. After considerable difficulty, the colonel managed to arrange a transfer for Massey to that hospital for surgery to repair the Briton's damaged leg. Two months after the transfer, von Lindeiner heard from the commandant of the camp where Massey was recovering. The Group Captain was apparently inciting his fellow prisoner-patients to mutiny and the hospital commandant was considering starting proceedings against Massey. He asked von Lindeiner if he would take Massey back into Stalag Luft III. The colonel agreed and had the British officer picked up and returned to Sagan. He later came to regret the trust he had placed in Massey.

Colonel von Lindeiner had high praise for two American officers in Luft III. Colonel Charles Goodrich had been seriously wounded when his aircraft was shot down over North Africa. Von Lindeiner referred to Goodrich as "a quiet, reserved gentleman who liked the company of books and who fulfilled his duties as senior officer of South Compound with the tact and understanding so characteristic of an American colonel." The commandant especially admired and respected Colonel Delmar Spivey, the American Senior Allied Officer during von Lindeiner's time of command. He felt that Spivey was a natural leader and knew well how to inspire, unite and discipline the men under his "command." Spivey's understanding and sensitivity, together with his ability to get things done, were complemented by his superior manners and his easy working relationship with the German camp administration. His rapport with von Lindeiner helped him to do all he could for the welfare and benefit of his men in that difficult situation. The commandant was convinced that all the Germans at Sagan who knew Colonel Spivey had a high regard for him.

In the dark, moonless night of 24th March 1944, what came to be known as "The Great Escape" took place. The carefully planned mass exit of 200 prisoners from Stalag Luft III, hut 104, Sagan, began around 10 p.m. The effort was immediately complicated when it was discovered that the tunnel constructed for it, which the POWs called 'Harry', actually emerged ten feet short of the woods. Various delays occurred during the night and were extended as some of the would-be escapees panicked while awaiting their turn in the claustrophobic tunnel. By 4 a.m., it was obvious that all of the 200 men selected for the attempt would not get out before the 5 a.m. deadline set by the escape committee.

Ultimately, 76 men got out through the tunnel to freedom. Of the total, only three men made it back to England. Twenty-three were recaptured and returned to Sagan, and on Hitler's orders fifty of the escapees were executed.

German investigators immediately arrived at Stalag Luft III. A day after the escape, von Lindeiner was relieved of duty as commandant of the camp. On 5th October, he was court martialed and convicted of failing to prevent the Great Escape. He was sentenced to twelve months confinement, but a military medical commission determined that the colonel suffered from "an advanced stage of mental disturbance" and ordered that he be admitted to an army hospital at Görlitz instead of prison. In April 1945, von Lindeiner became a prisoner, first of the Americans and then of the British, who imprisoned him for nearly two years. He died in 1963.

SOA, Stalag Luft I, Hub Zemke remembered the camp commander at Barth: "I was briefed that the camp Kommandant, Oberst Scherer, was an ardent Nazi, as were several members of his staff. In recent months the attitude toward prisoners had hardened, with the imposition of restrictive regulations backed by the threat of severe punishment on infringement.

"The Kommandant or his representative came to North I every Wednesday afternoon for a meeting with the Senior Allied Officer. Matters to be raised by the POWs had to be submitted in writing before the meetings. Most of our requests concerned seemingly mundane matters such as the provision of extra light bulbs, repair of a phonograph, a shortage of knives and forks, and the like. As my colleagues in Provisional Wing X had warned me, most of these requests were refused, often without reasonable explanation. But our hard-hearted would-be masters did relent over Christmas services, with permission for movement between some Lagers on the giving of paroles not to try to escape. In contrast to my lack of supporters—only the adjutant or a clerk could be present—the German staff usually appeared in strength at these meetings. Initially, I was aware that apart from Scherer himself, authority issued from a Major Schröder, who headed the Lager personnel, and Major von Miller zu Aichholz in charge of camp security. Both, I had been warned, were committed Nazis; von Miller in particular was detested for his actions against the POWs, especially in search and seizure raids.

"After only a couple of meetings new faces appeared in the camp administration. For reasons unknown to me, Scherer was transferred out and his place as Kommandant taken by an older man, Oberst von Warnstedt. At the same time there appears to have been a general shakeup in the staff, for other Luftwaffe officers disappeared, including Schröder. Unfortunately, the infamous von Miller remained to head the Abwehr detachment of security police.

"With the changed administration came new and ominous regulations. A new German order, issued soon after New Year's Day, warned that in future any prisoner touching a compound warning wire would be shot at without challenge. The warning wire was a single strand that ran knee-high around the inside of all compounds just inside the double barbed wire fence. As in the course of playing ball games or exercising it was quite easy for a prisoner to accidentally brush against the wire, this decree looked very much like a license for the guards to shoot at will. In another notice the new Lager Gruppenleiter (head of Lager personnel) Oberstleutnant Jäger announced the discontinuation of the regular Monday meetings between senior Allied officers and the Kommandant, which left only the Wednesday afternoon visit as a means of contact. Even more ominous in our minds was another requirement that all prisoners, both British and American, of the Jewish faith were to be housed in separate barracks in North I.

"This was not the end of the impositions making life more difficult for POWs. Officers were ordered to give up part of their bed linen so that this could be used by new prisoners who continued to arrive in large numbers, many removed from Stalag Luft IV at Gross Tychow to the east which was threatened by the Russian advance. Much furniture was also appropriated for use elsewhere. Most serious was that deliveries of foodstuffs from German sources, notably their potatoes, started to arrive late, sometimes a week overdue, causing reductions in daily rations. Additionally, a limit was put on the amount of food that an individual could save and store from his Red Cross parcels. Similarly the reserve of canned jam and other foods held by central compound stores was confiscated—and this at a time when the supply of Red Cross parcels held for the camp was down to a two weeks' supply.

"These inflictions, coming one after another, showed clearly that the new regime was deliberately turning the screw on our containment. Whether it was of their own volition or at the direction of higher authority we had no way of telling.

"Our immediate recourse was to write to the Representative of our Protective Power, which happened to be the Swiss legation in Germany, protesting that our jailers had violated articles in the Geneva Convention. The representative visited the camp every six months and, as he had been there just two days before my arrival, was not scheduled again until April. In the letter we requested that the seriousness of the matters outlined required an immediate visit. Although the Germans, as signatories to the 1929 Geneva Convention on the rights of prisoners of war, were obliged to forward the letter, on past showing it was likely they would sit on it for a month or so—which they did.

"Faced with this oppression, it was in the nature of the American prisoners to show their defiance in any way they could. While the Headquarters staff of Provisional Wing X would secretly encourage and support this resistance, it was important that they maintain what dialogue there was with our oppressors. Protest and demand, but never stoop to measures that would discredit our standing as the mouthpiece and authority of the POWs. In consequence I did not lose an opportunity to request an audience with the Kommandant.

"While the majority of our grievances were turned aside and I had to rely on the one weekly meeting to get my points across, gradually it did seem they were receiving more attention, even if mostly in the negative sense. Despite the harsh regulations he had imposed, or been instructed to impose, von Warnstedt did not mostly in the negative sense. Despite the harsh regulations he had imposed, or been instructed to impose, von Warnstedt did not appear to be a hard-core Nazi disciplinarian. One distinct advantage I had was being able to converse in German, if haltingly, as this allowed direct exchanges with the Kommandant, avoiding the filtering of an interpreter. He came over as a man who was not enthusiastic about the job he held down, the more so because other members of his staff appeared to speak for him or he would pass my question to one of them. In fact, I had an had an inkling that he was a little disenchanted with the war and, if I sensed correctly, he was not the only member of his staff so affected."

From the Geneva Convention relative to the treatment of prisoners of war: Article 39 requires a PW camp to be under the immediate authority of a responsible commissioned officer of the regular armed forces of the detaining power, and requires him to possess a copy of the Convention and insure that its provisions are known to the camp staff. Article 41 requires that the text of the Convention be made known to PWs, and Article 42 restricts the use of weapons against prisoners. Recognition of PW rank and promotions in rank is required by the detaining power under articles 43-44. Articles 46-48 specify detailed requirements as to the conditions under which PWs may be transferred, and provide that PWs may take with them their personal effects not in excess of 25 kilograms (55 pounds) per person. The conditions under which the detaining power may utilize the labor of PWs are set forth in Articles 49-57. Noncommissioned officers shall only be required to to supervisory work. Officers may not be compelled to work, but may ask to do so.

Article 82 (Penal and Disciplinary Sanctions) provides that acts punishable by the laws of the detaining power, but which are not punishable if committed by a member of that state's forces, shall entail only disciplinary punishment. This provision is reinforced by Article 87, which excludes the application to PWs of any penalties other than those provided for the same acts in respect of members of the armed forces of the detaining power. No PW may be tried or sentenced for an act which is not forbidden by the law of the detaining power or by international law in force at the time the act was committed (Article 99).

ESCAPE

IT WAS THE DUTY of an airman, American or British, officer or noncom, who was brought down over Europe and was physically undamaged, to avoid capture by the enemy and, if he were captured, to escape. His thoughts should always be directed to getting back to his base and returning to the fight. Far away in eastern Europe, in the depths of winter, surrounded by a hostile population, with no knowledge of the language, no civilian credentials, the wrong kind of clothing and no food, the prospects of evasion might seem a little slim; nevertheless, many airmen tried it, and a surprising number did make it. But the problems of escaping over, through or under the barbed wire fences of a well-guarded prison camp were of a different order. Still, tens of thousands of POWs devoted all their energies and thoughts to it, hundreds contrived it, some of them several times. Most were recaptured, but they had fulfilled their duty, and every breakout caused a big diversion of enemy resources.

Everyone knew that the best way to escape, and by far the least tiring, was to walk out through the gate. It was also the hardest to contrive: you needed the disguise, and the papers, at least a smattering of the language and a whole lot of nerve. It was the method employed on more than one occasion by Warrant Officer George Grimson, but Grimson, "the ace escaper" was a man of exceptional resourcefulness. If one's passing through the gate was difficult, then going through the wire verged on the suicidal, and going over it really lay in the realm of fantasy—although a few remarkable attempts were made. The best prospects—and even they were pretty slim—lay underground. The tunnel must be deep enough for the sound of digging to be unheard on the surface, and to remain undiscovered by the ferrets' probes; it must also be long enough to reach whatever shelter lay beyond the wire.

The number of escapes that were attempted will never be accurately known, but it quite is certain that there were many thousands. Although the hard fact is that few were successful— only 156 RAF men, for example, made a 'home run'—that cannot be taken as a measure of their worth.

Although most POWs constantly dreamed of escaping, studied it and worked for it, day after day, month after month, when it came to the crunch, when the time came for the breakout, the prospect did not always seem quite as attractive as it had been in the planning. It was then that you realised how fragile your disguise was, how suspect your papers, how inadequate your rations, your knowledge of the language, your stamina, your strength.

When at last RAF pilot Robert Kee's turn came to take part in an escape attempt (which involved the use of a home-made ladder and sabotage of the Stalag's power supply), he suddenly felt qualms about the enterprise. "All manner of hopeless thoughts attacked me," he wrote. "I began to feel sentimental about the familiar squalor, and I should be quite content, I thought, to live here for ever, smelling the cooking and the lavatory and the dust, looking forward to my two slices of bread at lunch or tea and my Red Cross stew at supper, thinking about all the books I am going to read and how nice it is going to be when I can speak German and Russian fluently. I only want to be allowed to live, and enjoy the sun when it shines, and wait for it when it goes behind a cloud."

This plan, as it happened, was basically unsound, with every prospect of disaster, and it was probably as well for Kee and his companions that, despite the sabotage, the guard box searchlights continued to function, albeit intermittently, and the attempted breakout was aborted. It was sometime later that Kee, with forty other men, tunneled their way out of that Stalag.

Oflag IX, in Spangenburg Castle twenty miles south of Kassel, was the scene of a notable escape attempt in September 1942. Breaking into a room in one of the castle's turrets, three British prisoners discovered an Oberleutnant's uniform as well as some civilian clothes.

They decided to assume the role of the members of a Swiss mission who, with a German officer as escort, were making an official visit to the Oflag. Accompanied by two German-speaking prisoners, who maintained a continuing conversation with them, they approached the gate. There, they exchanged farewells with their "escort", acknowledged the guard's salute, and marched away. In the cover of the woods, they removed their outer clothing and emerged as three officers of the German Air Force. Aidan Crawley takes up the story: "Having unsuccessfully tried two airfields near Kassel, hoping to steal an aircraft . . . they decided to turn west towards Cologne. By living on apples and vegetables they travelled more than a hundred miles before their luck deserted them. A solitary sentry in a village, though ignorant of what a German Air Force uniform looked like, became suspicious of their dress. He alleged, wrongly, that the caps were made incorrectly, but explanation proved too much for the prisoner's grasp of German and they were arrested. Each received a sentence of 52 days in solitary confinement."

It was in the business of escape and evasion that fliers of the USAAF, the RAF and Commonwealth Air Forces had an advantage over other Allied airmen: the authorities in Britain and, in due course, in America, realized that every POW had the potential to be a major nuisance to the enemy, and set up the machinery—MI9 in London and MIS-X in Washington—to help him be exactly that.

These small departments, staffed by hand-picked teams of innovative, energetic officers, co-operated closely from the early days of 1942, when the MIS-X men were glad to make use of MI9's two years' experience—an approach in which they differed from some high-ranking members of the American armed forces, who stoutly declined to take any account of what the Britishers had learned, and promptly proceeded to make all the same mistakes again.

Soon after General Carl Spaatz arrived to command the USAAF in England, he directed W. Stull Holt of Johns Hopkins University to work alongside Colonel Norman Crockett, the head of MI9. Holt's brief, which was similar to Crockett's, was to receive escape kits from the British and issue them to all Spaatz's fliers, to prepare and execute plans for the escape of American POWs, to instruct selected combat crewmen in the use of codes, and to elicit information from POWs by correspondence in those codes.

"We spent the summer days walking inside the wire and digging escape tunnels," said Don Ackerson. "The soil at Barth was sandy and disposal of the sand was a problem. We would tie a sock inside our pants leg and let it sift through a hole in the sock to the ground as we walked. The tunnels all went from under a barracks out under the wire toward the woods. There was always a dummy tunnel, dug first and only out fifteen feet or so, while the real tunnel went parallel to it. One cross-eyed guard started digging outside the barracks—lining himself up with the discovered tunnel—and dug into the real one by lining himself up crooked. The real tunnel, which he dug into, was only a few feet from the woods at that time. Tunnels and other escape attempts and plans kept us busy. We did as much as possible to keep the Germans occupied."

It was when the NCO prisoners at Stalag Luft I were transferred to III that George Grimson embarked on the series of breakouts, sometimes in company, other times alone, which would earn him the name of "ace escaper". Twice he got away posing as a German (he had taught himself the language during his imprisonment), only to be recaptured and sentenced to solitary confinement on a diet of only bread and water in the Sagan "cooler". On another attempt, dressed in "borrowed" overalls and a German forage cap, Grimson, carrying a ladder and a dummy electric meter, approached a guard box on the camp perimeter. "Testing the telephone lines," he informed the guard, and climbed over the wire, applying his box of tricks to the cable here and there. Apparently satisfied, he was moving away into the Vorlager—the administration compound—when the guard remonstrated: "You must go out the same way you came in!" "Don't be silly. I'm not walking all through the camp when my billet's just over there," said Grimson, and strolled on. He was recaptured five days later on the train to Stettin and brought back to the cooler, but Grimson was by no means finished yet.

In June 1943, Sagan's NCO POWs (except for fifty volunteers who stayed as orderlies for the incoming USAAF officer prisoners) were transferred to a new camp at Heydekrug on the Baltic coast, and it was not long before Grimson was on his way again, and this time he was never to return. He knew that an escaper, scruffy, dirty, haggard and unshaven, was likely to be noticed by a sharp-eyed member of the Hitler Youth, and certainly by a policeman or a serviceman. His intention was to establish a point-to-point escape route with a chain of "safe houses" where a man could rest and clean up, and to maintain contact with the escape committee by regular meetings outside Heydekrug with the German camp interpreter, Munkert, who had proved himself a true friend to the prisoners.

Grimson's travels took him to all the Baltic sea-ports from Lubeck to Memel, looking for helpers, possible safe-houses, and a friendly ship's captain who might offer passage to a neutral port. He settled on Danzig, where he found a set of rooms, laid in a stock of food, obtained a harbour pass and access to a rowing boat. He set up a rendezvous and a system of signals for those who were to follow his route out. He could have made his own escape at any time—indeed he was ordered to do so in April 1944 by the escape committee—but he seems to have seen it as his duty to remain in Germany, playing the role of a World War II Scarlet Pimpernel. Then he disappeared, and no-one truly knows what happened to George Grimson. There were reports that the Gestapo had at last caught up with him; another, that he had made his way to Russia and elected to remain there. One thing is certain: he has no known grave. Douglas Connolly, who knew him, said "I didn't really like him—he was a bit of a loner. But he was a fantastic bloke".

Another successful escaper was the Yorkshireman Richard Pape, a pre-war journalist and German-speaker, who was the navigator of a No. 15 Squadron Stirling bomber which crash-landed in Holland on the way back from a Berlin raid on the night of 7th September 1941. After some weeks in hiding with the Dutch underground movement, Pape was captured, brutally interrogated, and imprisoned at Stalag VIIIB, Lamsdorf, near the Polish border. During the next three years, Pape made an extraordinary sequence of escapes from working parties, adopting the identity of a New Zealand private soldier.

When "Big X"—the head of the Sagan escape committee—at last permitted Eric Lapham to join in a tunnelling attempt, he jumped at the chance. "The project," he remembered, "was based on the creation of a small chamber under the soakaway in the ablution floor. The ablution had to remain unused, but be sufficiently damp to allay suspicion because of the British tendency to encourage novice musicians while insisting that they practised in ablutions or latrines. The advantage of our ablution was that it straddled the no-man's land between the warning boards and the boundary wire.

My task was to carry vessels full of excavated sand from the ablution to our hut. There it was either scattered out of the window or loaded into bags hung inside people's trousers and gradually discharged as they walked around the camp."

Like so many, this project failed. Sagan was swamped by a sudden summer storm, and the "Scheissen Wagon"—the horse-drawn cart which weekly collected human waste from the ablutions—slowly sank through the sand and laid the tunnel bare. Such calamities were not uncommon. They invariably resulted in a gathering of agitated ferrets, troops of guards with rifles at the ready, a grim line of hard-eyed men in black hats and long macintoshes, and an immediate appell. The reaction of the Commandant and his lieutenants would vary from spluttering fury, through icy condemnation, to simulated disappointment—how could any officer demonstrate such gross ingratitude for German hospitality.

The "Great Escape" by seventy POWs from the North Camp at Sagan in March 1944 has been the subject of numerous books and a fine, if not entirely factual, motion picture. It was a remarkable enterprise that was brilliantly planned mainly by Roger Bushell, the clever archetypal "Big X", and executed with extraordinary determination. The labours of the tunnellers, the skills of the carpenters, the forgers, the tailors and mechanics need no embellishment here. The dreadful ending only offers further proof that the brutal regime which ordered it had to be brought down.

In *Exemplary Justice* the author Allen Andrews gives a chilling account of how General Artur Nebe, the Kripo chief at RSHA in Berlin, selected the recaptured officers for clandestine murder by the Gestapo. "I gave Nebe the personal file cards," said one of his aides. "Each contained a photograph and personal details of the officer concerned. He sorted the cards into two piles, saying 'He is for it' and 'He is so young' and 'Children? No'. When he had a stack of fifty, as ordered by Himmler, he handed it to me, saying 'Make a list of those. Quickly'."

Winston Churchill, speaking in the British House of Commons in June 1944, stated his resolve that "these foul criminals shall be tracked down. They will be brought to exemplary justice." He was as good as his word. A dedicated unit of the RAF's Special

Investigation, led by Wing Commander Wilfrid Bowes, in a three-year search, identified seventy-two of the murderers and brought sixty-nine to book. Few other governments would have been quite so obdurate: the Russians, for their part, and the east Europeans regarded the death of the fifty officers as hardly meriting a fuss, and of course it pales in comparison with many wartime instances of slaughter and brutality by the Nazi thugs, with the brutal SS massacre at Oradour-sur-Glane, the Polish thousands gunned down at Katyn, the killing grounds of Warsaw, and the mass exterminations in the concentration camps.

Colonel Spivey, Senior Allied Officer, Center Compound, Sagan, remembered: "One major phase of German camp administration was the employment of guards who continuously patrolled the interior of the compounds on the lookout for evidence of escape activities. These guards were called the 'ferrets' by the prisoners. Needless to say, they were not popular. A few weeks after my arrival I noticed from my window, which faced the playground and from which I could see both cookhouses and most of the barracks, five or six men scurrying between the kitchen and their barracks, carrying pitchers full of boiling water. This was unusual, since it was not tea time or meal time. I concluded they must be carrying water to scrub the barracks. About five minutes later, the German Abwehr sergeant who was in charge of ferrets burst into my room in the greatest possible state of excitement. I had had several conversations with this man and, as with the Kommandant, had agreed on a procedure for dealing with trouble in my camp. In all cases other than escapes I was to be consulted before the Abwehr took any direct action. And so, in keeping with this understanding, he had come to find me. Only a German would have kept his word under similar circumstances.

At his urgent request I followed him at a dead run to the barracks into which the hot water had been flowing so rapidly. There I found the greatest imaginable commotion. The barracks, which was built on pillars about three feet tall to allow searching parties to go under the floor, was practically empty except for eight or ten Kriegies madly dashing boiling water on the floor and yelling such incoherent phrases as 'Here's the SOB!' 'More water!' 'Teach the bastard a lesson!' 'Scald him!' 'Don't let the skunk escape!' 'Watch the exit!' and so on. The German sergeant was too excited and angry to talk, so I ordered a halt to the procedure and was greeted with 'Why in hell did you have to appear just when we were having a little fun?' Then they explained they had caught a ferret eavesdropping under the barracks and were merely teaching him to mind his own business. The poor ferret was in agony and in mortal fear for his life since he couldn't escape without exposing himself to a full pitcher of scalding water. Nor could he defend himself since he wasn't allowed to carry arms in the camp. So he was trying to change his position under the barracks often enough to avoid being drenched. This incident and many to follow could have resulted in severe disciplinary action had it not been for the good relations we had at that time with the German camp administration.

"One's first impulse upon being shot down was to escape. That impulse remained with nearly everyone until he was successful in escaping or was freed. It became an obsession with some; to others it was a faint hope after the first shock of failure and the rude awakening to the almost insurmountable difficulties facing an imprisoned officer of the USAAF. But to all of us the desire to be free was ever present. From the very beginning, the officers of the RAF and the USAAF had the dubious honor of being valued more highly by the Germans than any other category of war prisoner. In consequence, we were guarded more closely than than any other group.

"The German security system was simple and extremely effective. All they did was to put us in a well-built barbed wire enclosure along which were guard towers ('goon boxes') about twenty feet high, manned constantly by more or less alert guards armed with machine-guns, rifles, pistols, and huge, powerful search lights.

Under the fence they buried a series of seismographic instruments designed to record in a central office any disturbance created by tunneling activities in the vicinity of the fence. On the outside of the enclosure were roving guards by night and watchers by day, hidden in piles of brush, observing our activities. The patrol guards were accompanied by well-trained and vicious police dogs. On the inside by day we had our ever-present ferret, or unarmed Abwehr guards, stalking over every inch of the place, walking unannounced into barracks, crawling in the attics and under the barracks, and remaining hidden in attic or basement for hours on end. They dressed in coveralls, professed to speak no English, plodded around with their hands behind their backs observing everything which went on, and alert to anything that looked suspicious. During the night the ferrets came and went as directed. At sunset we were locked in our barracks; one or two guards with dogs patrolled within the camp throughout the night.

"To counter these efficient security measures we organized our own escape organization, referred to as 'X'. Before 1943, escape was not a highly organized camp undertaking but rather was the product of a few individuals who dreamed up and tried to put into effect schemes of their own. The British found that this procedure was ineffective, so they carefully selected and trained people in specialized phases of the escape program. When I came to Center Compound from North, I brought along a staff to organize the camp so it would make life easier for us and would function to the satisfaction of the Germans. This was a big help to the Germans since it relieved them of having to keep a large number of recalcitrant POWs in solitary confinement. Also it helped them in accounting for Reich property within the camp. I am certain the Germans knew that this staff had been trained in 'X' work, but the German record at preventing escapes was so good that they didn't seem too worried by our activities."

Barry Mahon, another guest of the Germans at Stalag Luft III, remembered an escape attempt: "Skinner and I were given priority to be included in the very next escape of one kind or another. At this point Wally Floody, one of my roommates in the first camp, had been appointed head engineer on the tunnels made famous in the book and movie about The Great Escape. He asked me to work with him. Since I had no previous experience on tunnels, I was put into the dispersement section. This meant carrying sand that was dug up during the day—carrying it in pockets designed out of sleeves of overcoat lining fastened inside your pants legs. As you walked around the camp you pulled a little string, allowing the new sand to be mixed lightly with the old.

"These three tunnels, if I remember correctly, extended a total of 300 hundred feet. They were 25 feet underground and were at least 2 feet square, and there were several collection, dispersal and air pump chambers. I never went into the tunnels myself.

"While plans for the tunnels were progressing, the X Committee developed a special project, mainly to ridicule the Germans and their ambitions for an escape-proof prison. Thirty of us would walk right out the front gate.

"On account of our previous disappointment with the trucks and trees, Skinner and I were approached and included in a so-called delousing party. The plan consisted first of discovering a louse in one of the American barracks, and then putting into motion the German rule that the whole barracks must be deloused immediately. This meant that we prisoners had to be marched under guard out of the compound to delousing showers some distance down the road. I am not quite sure where they found this louse, but it was planted in the bedclothing of one of the boys and promptly shown to the Germans.

"Before this, through much careful planning, two German uniforms had been manufactured using RAF material covered with talcum powder to make it a proper gray color. Certain pieces of ribbon, piping, and insignia had been collected from German enlisted men under the guise of souvenir swapping. From these originals, casts were made out of cigarette-pack tin foil that had been collected by the thousands. Enough lead or aluminum was melted to pour into the molds and make genuine-looking buttons and insignia.

"A Polish woodworker also had made two replicas of German rifles, down to the detail of an actual working bolt and breech mechanism. These wooden models had been colored by shoe polish and absolutely could not be distinguished from the original. Because the escape was to be accomplished in our own uniforms, we were not required to go through much briefing of our crew.

"On the day the louse was discovered, all preparations had been completed. It was arranged that the delousing parades would start the next morning with the whole maneuver tied to the hour at which the sentries on duty at the main gate changed shifts.

"Escorted by two German guards, our first delousing group left the camp on schedule with belongings tied up in sheets and blankets to be fumigated. As planned, this group of prisoners would be docile and obedient, with no attempt to escape, in order to lull the German escorts into a false sense of security. The trick now was to delay the new set of guards coming into the camp to escort the second delousing group to the showers, long enough to involve a new set of gate sentries just coming on duty. We members of the second POW group were the ones assigned to make the actual escape.

"As the German escorts for our second delousing group arrived in camp, our adjutant took them into a room across the compound, saying that the delousing group was not quite ready and would the escorts like some good American coffee, compliments of the Red Cross, plus a piece of pie and maybe a cigar. These items were irresistible to the Germans. They had not seen real coffee or cigars for four or five years.

"When the sentries on the gate had changed shifts, the two escort guards were informed that their little party was ready and would assemble shortly. In the meantime two of our German-speaking prisoners—one was Norwegian and the other a Czech—had dressed in the fake uniforms and they led our delousing group right out through the main gate.

"Since the sentries now at the gate, having just arrived, were not aware of the German escorts who were enjoying coffee and pie with our adjutant, we walked past them and out of the camp without a hitch. As soon as we were clear, and well down the road, our fellow prisoners still inside the camp assembled the real shower parade and called the two real German escort guards out of the coffee klatsch.

"Now the gate sentries were a bit confused. Their records showed that only two escorting guards had come in the gates, and now the number going out would be four. But since the guards coming out at this point were legitimate, the new sentries marked the mix-up down to an oversight on the part of the previous sentry team, and they allowed this parade to leave in the direction of the showers.

"Meanwhile, our group had continued down the road just far enough to get out of sight. Instead of going on into the German part of the camp for our showers, we broke and headed for the woods, shepherded by our two phony escorts. Not until evening, when the books at the gate still showed one shower parade missing, did it dawn on the Germans that 30 officers had walked out through the main gate of what they considered an escape-proof camp. There were 10,000 Allied officers in the camp enjoying the biggest laugh they had since they had been in Germany.

"Skinner and I immediately changed our uniforms to those of French workers. Not much of a change; merely putting on a beret and wearing a French overcoat. We continued walking south that day and on through the night through a reforestation area, and actually saw no one for the first 60 or 70 miles. We headed toward Czechoslovakia and followed a railroad that our map indicated would take us in the right direction.

"The next day about noon we came upon a quarry being mined by British enlisted-men war prisoners. We practically walked into the middle of this thing before we realized where we were. We turned and went slowly up the hill, hoping that no one would notice. Once on top of the hill, there was no exit. We were so tired we dropped in our tracks and slept several hours. We were awakened by a gentle rain and looked down to find the quarry empty.

"This much concentrated walking had caused both of us to develop all kinds of foot ailments, including very deep blisters. After this deep sleep we found that our muscles would not operate at all. Helping each other to a sitting position, and eventually standing, took 15 to 20 minutes of sheer pain. About the only way we could get started was to propel our bodies forward and let self-preservation make the muscles work. After a while the kinks were out and we were walking normally again.

"We were cutting through a wheat field when we heard voices almost directly in front of us. We dropped in our tracks, and soon figured it was a German man and woman dallying in the green. He was giving her every phony argument that any soldier has ever used to overcome her resistance. The seduction took several hours. It was hard for us to contain our laughter. When finally the two had left, we continued on across the field and picked up a road that we believed would take us into Czechoslovakia.

"This particular evening the moon was out and the walking was easy. However, because of our fatigue, we stayed to the road instead of cutting through fields as we should have done. As we got to a settlement neat the border, we found ourselves unexpectedly inside the village, with no chance of turning back. There were several

below: John Hurd, a B-17 sergeant gunner before and after capture by the Germans; bottom: The double barbed wire fence at Stalag Luft III, Sagan, Silesia, in 1944.

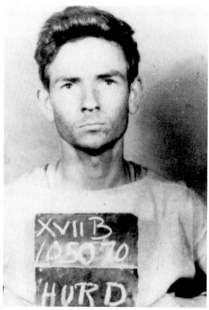

below left: An RAF airman is escorted to prison camp; below right: The Dulag Luft interrogator Hanns Scharff; bottom: An aerial view of Stalag Luft III, Sagan, in 1944.

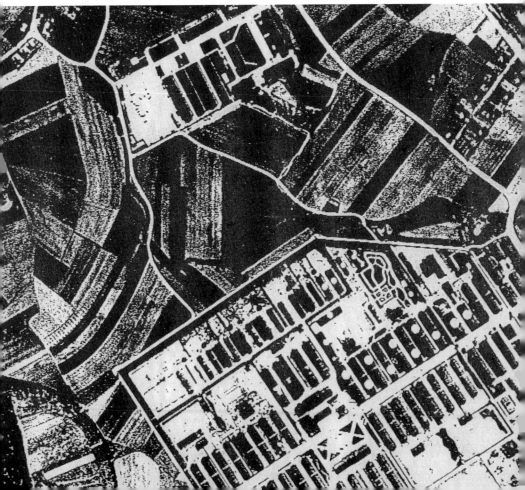

Of all the daily concerns endured by the Allied prisoners of Nazi Germany, probably none was more oppressive than not knowing how long their incarceration would last.

top: British prisoners at Sagan preparing part of their meal, incorporating items from Red Cross parcels; above: Part of the Stalag Luft III guard contingent; right: Kriegies gathered to hear music by a small prisoner orchestra whose instruments were provided by the International YMCA.

top: Col. Friedrich-Wilhelm von Lindeiner-Wildau, commandant, Stalag Luft III, Sagan, at the time of the Great Escape; above: The 'cooler', solitary confinement at Stalag Luft III.

below: The appell, or roll call, at one of the compounds in Stalag Luft III, Sagan, in 1944. The continuing informal harassment campaign by the kriegies against their captors often resulted in a miscount at these routine assemblies.

73. Albert Drive.
August 3rd 1940.
Saturday.

Dearest Joe.

So be able to write to you once more is wonderful. No matter how far off you are. at least one day you will come back. We have had such a fright. the last months have been almost unbearable. I wont dwell on them.

Dont be too sad will you. I am still waiting just for you. Everyone has been so nice, all enquiring after you. I have to send love from all aunts etc but most of all from Lily, Fred, Iris. Mother. Dad. John. they will be as happy as I to see you. Think of our future Joe, we will make up for all troubles. I dont think I could love you more than I do. sometimes in the past weeks I have thought my heart would break. Life for you will be hard I guess, many of us will be thinking of you always. Your family have been so good. all writing. your father has written

left: May Jordan, fiancé of Private Joe Butcher who was captured at Dunkirk and spent more than four years behind the wire in Germany; above: A letter from May to Joe at Stalag XXa.

top: A sports day organized by RAF prisoners at Stalag Luft III, Sagan; above: A band made up of RAF prisoners believed to be at Stalag Luft I, Barth; right: A crap game in one of the stalags, 1943.

below: American Red Cross volunteers packing food parcels for delivery to POWs in Germany; bottom: Relatives and friends of American POWs learning what they may send to their boys.

To all Prisoners of War!

The escape from prison camps is no longer a sport!

Germany has always kept to the Hague Convention and only punished recaptured prisoners of war with minor disciplinary punishment.

Germany will still maintain these principles of international law.

But England has besides fighting at the front in an honest manner instituted an illegal warfare in non combat zones in the form of gangster commandos, terror bandits and sabotage troops even up to the frontiers of Germany.

They say in a captured secret and confidential English military pamphlet,

Red ↓

THE HANDBOOK
OF MODERN IRREGULAR
WARFARE:

". . . the days when we could practise the rules of sportsmanship are over. For the time being, every soldier must be a potential gangster and must be prepared to adopt their methods whenever necessary."

Red ↓

"The sphere of operations should always include the enemy's own country, any occupied territory, and in certain circumstances, such neutral countries as he is using as a source of supply."

England has with these instructions opened up a non military form of gangster war!

Germany is determined to safeguard her homeland, and especially her war industry and provisional centres for the fighting fronts. Therefore it has become necessary to create strictly forbidden zones, called death zones, in which all unauthorised trespassers will be immediately shot on sight.

Escaping prisoners of war, entering such death zones, will certainly lose their lives. They are therefore in constant danger of being mistaken for enemy agents or sabotage groups.

Urgent warning is given against making future escapes!

In plain English: Stay in the camp where you will be safe! Breaking out of it is now a damned dangerous act.

Red ↓

The chances of preserving your life are almost nil!

All police and military guards have been given the most strict orders to shoot on sight all suspected persons.

Escaping from prison camps has ceased to be a sport!

top: In the final months of the war, many POWs were led by their captors on a forced march west, away from the advancing Russians.

top: Krieigies awaiting liberation at Moosberg in the final days of the war; above: Liberation at the Moosburg camp in the form of General George Patton's 3rd Army came on 19 April 1945.

top: An American Red Cross worker offers advice and suggestions to newly liberated POWs at Camp Lucky Strike near Le Havre, France, in 1945.

guards along the road, in the German custom. We had passed two of them and were almost clear of the town when a third guard, quite elderly, stopped us. We told him we were Hungarian workers, but he took us to the Burgermeister, the mayor of the town. They searched us and found our escape rations, our dog tags, our map. "The whole police network of Germany had been alerted about our escape, and the old guard who captured us was an instant hero. I imagine it would have been easy for us to have pushed him into the river. He was armed with a giant revolver that probably would have exploded had he tried to fire it. But our orders were to get out as cleanly as possible, without violence, in order to maintain our status as escaped POWs, rather than wanted criminals. Escaped prisoners were returned to their establishment, while criminals would be taken by the Gestapo or the police.

"We were driven to the next village, a large railhead. Eventually two guards came to get us. Since it was an evening train trip, they were allowed to bring their wives. On the return to Sagan, the conductor locked the four of them and two of us into a compartment.

"One of the women spoke a certain amount of English, and Skinner and I knew just enough German to carry on a halting conversation. The talk evolved around our camp, which the woman said must be Utopia, full of sugar, coffee, cigarettes, and other luxuries. She said she could not understand why we should want to escape when our lot in camp was so much better than that of the average German civilian.

"Not wishing to go into the political or military considerations, I told her I wanted to escape because I missed my mother very much. That was true, of course, but not on the exact sentimental scale that I had sounded. Germans of this middle class are very family-conscious. As my remarks sank into her mind, tears came into her eyes and she began to deride her poor husband. 'It is shameful that these fine young men are being held in camps.' she said. The husband looked at me and shrugged his shoulders and said in German, 'Why did you have to get her started on something like that?'

"We were taken back to camp and given 14 days of solitary confinement."

From the Geneva Convention relative to the treatment of prisoners of war: Articles 91-95 detail the consequences of attempted escapes and define the conditions which must be met before an escape can be regarded as successful (Article 91), an important provision because of the effects produced by a successful escape. Article 96 prohibits camp commanders from delegating their disciplinary powers to PWs, and requires a record to be kept of disciplinary punishments open to inspection by representatives of the protecting power.

EVADERS

THE DIFFERENCE between an evader and an escaper is that the evader contrives not to get captured by the enemy. Nearly two thousand RAF fliers were successful in evading capture.

Flying Officer Ronald Hawkins of No.103 Squadron was one of those rare individuals who was both an escaper and an evader. In the early evening of 14th June 1940, he had taken off in a single-engined Fairey Battle of the British Advanced Air Striking Force from an airfield in France to attack units of the German Army located in a forest south-west of Evreux. Despite being attacked by eleven Me-109s while at 8,000 feet on his approach to the target, he pressed on and dropped his bombs on the enemy positions. By now, his cockpit was on fire, his controls had gone, and the Battle was in a dive. He ordered his crewman, Pilot Officer Hugill, to jump and, with some difficulty, made his own exit.

"I pulled the ripcord immediately," he wrote in his subsequent report to his Squadron Commander, "and regretted it at once as I was given a few bursts of fire. I hung limp, shamming that I'd been hit. Hugill was floating down several miles away and I have not seen him since. My aircraft and one of the 109s crashed fairly near the target—the 109 was presumably shot down by Hugill, possibly helped by the bursts I gave them from the front guns whenever they went by the nose after attacking."

Hawkins landed safely, hid his parachute and, lying low in a cornfield to the west of the forest, watched the soldiers searching for him through the trees. All that night and the next, he travelled southward by the stars. Then, hungry and thirsty, he was trying to find water in a farmyard when he was captured by a German patrol. "I was driven to a sub-headquarters," his report continued, "given breakfast, taken to a unit near Vernon and interrogated. I gave my name, rank and number, but managed to pick up the piece of paper on which the interrogator had written this as I left his office. From there I was taken to a former French barracks and put with about 500 French prisoners. The food was quite reasonable and the treatment good. The captain allowed us to enter the stores and to help ourselves to kit, so I obtained a haversack, water bottle, hammer, chisel, a pair of pliers and a file while no-one was looking."

After two days in this relaxed environment, the prisoners were taken to a camp near Evreux. This consisted of a flour mill and adjoining house which the Germans used as offices and living quarters, an open field for the French other ranks (by now some 2,000 troops), and an outhouse for thirty or so officers. The camp was surrounded by barbed wire and machine gun posts, and was bordered on the south by a river. Having tried without success to encourage the other British officers—three Army and one RAF—to join in the attempt, Hawkins made his escape in the early hours of 19th June by crawling to the river along a sewage drain, moving only when the sentries' backs were turned.

It was at this point that Hawkins made what appears to have been his only error of judgement. Calculating that the river was so shallow that he could wade across, he removed his trousers, and lost them (with his money) when he found he had to swim. Resourceful as ever, he whipped off his shirt, wrung it out, put his feet through the sleeves and marched on west towards the coast.

"I reached Trouville," he reported, "on June 22nd, and was given old civilian clothes and some bread and sugar by a farmer, having lived on biscuits saved from prison camp, supplemented by potatoes from the fields and milk when I could find a friendly cow."

Although he searched the coast eastward from Trouville to le Tréport, he could find no boat in which to row across the Channel as he hoped. Turning south-west again, he was relieved to find an unattended bicycle, as his shoes were holed and his feet were badly blistered. Begging and stealing food along the way, he reached Carteret—the nearest point to one of the British Channel Islands—on 30th June. "I obtained a canvas canoe," his report continued, "and steered a rough star course for Jersey, landed there on July 1st and was given food and drink, but told that the enemy had occupied the island that day, so returned to the mainland that night."

On another stolen bicycle, the indomitable Hawkins next set course for Vichy, where he arrived on 11th July. A very helpful Frenchman gave him 50 francs, which he spent on informing his parents by cablegram that he was "safe". Unsurprisingly (for America was then a neutral country), he received little help from Vichy's US Consul, and only escaped internment by making a rapid departure. He reached Marseilles on 16th July and, carrying an empty crate, boarded the only neutral ship in the docks. The Greek skipper was friendly but had no sailing orders. He might, he thought, not leave for several months. Hawkins turned next to the British Consulate, hoping to obtain money for a Spanish visa. The best that the benighted office clerks could provide was less than a third of the 1,000 francs he needed.

He passed a few nights in a seaman's hostel, until the gendarmes arrived to take the British inmates away for internment. Another hasty exit, and he was on the train for Perpignan. From there he travelled by road to the foothills of the Pyrenees and, in the night of 27th July, he crossed the frontier into Spain. From there, via Barcelona and Madrid, with the assistance of Sir Samuel Hoare, the British Ambassador, Hawkins at last reached British territory in Gibraltar on 23rd September, and was back in England two weeks later.

In due course, he returned to operational duties, in command of No. 3 Squadron, which was then based in Kent, flying Hawker Typhoon fighter-bombers. Squadron Leader Ronald Hawkins, MC AFC, was killed in action leading his squadron on a mission to Belgium on 5th October 1943.

The courageous civilians who helped Allied airmen to evade capture in Occupied Europe wittingly did so at the hazard of their own lives. As has been recorded in an earlier chapter, Johan Vierbergenweg, the brave young Dutchman from Oudewater, was caught when assisting Eric Lapham and his pilot to escape. His fate, as witnessed by a Wehrmacht interpreter, a Dutch-speaking German, and described in a post-war letter to Johan's father, may stand as a tribute to all who made that sacrifice.

"At 4 o'clock on Friday morning, 11th February 1944, I had to appear in a room of the military gaol, together with the military judge, a civil lawyer and a priest. Your son was brought in and as far as I remember, he was dressed in civilian clothes, a brown coat, grey trousers and black boots. His hair was well brushed and he was clean shaven. The judge read out the conviction. After that your son with his lawyer was allowed to appeal to a higher court. His official appeal was immediately considered by that court, though not to his advantage.

"Your son was convicted for helping in the endeavour of two English officers in 1943, whom he had met while he himself was in hiding from the Germans. Your son pleaded 'Not guilty'.

"For about an hour, while the appeal was being considered, your son was left alone with the priest. After that he was soon informed by the judge through me that his appeal had failed. When the judge then offered to shake hands with him, your son proudly refused. Before we were parted I had the opportunity of speaking a few comforting words to him, who had so bravely accepted his conviction.

"At 8 o'clock the judges and I arrived at the place of execution, the policeman wanted to blindfold him, but your son refused this. He stood there upright and proud and kissed the crucifix, which the priest held.

"I spoke the last words to him and said: 'You are a brave young man and your family and country may be proud of you'. Your son shook hands with me and said: 'I like to shake hands with you. I could not do that with the officer this morning, who is to me the representative of injustice. I thank you for your comforting and kindly words'.

After that he gave me your address and I had to retire. Before the command was given to fire, your son called aloud: 'Long live Holland'.

Shot by ten bullets, he died immediately."

Many years later, a thoroughfare in Johan's home town of Oudewater was officially renamed "Johan Vierbergenweg".

Bill Harvey flew B-17s with the 384th Bomb Group based at Grafton Underwood. He had been assigned to train new crews and get them ready for flying their combat tours. He describes his final mission: "In those days in England you had to fly 25 missions which was your tour of duty, then you could go home. I had been looking at that magic number for months. I had been in the group longer than any of the flying personnel other than some squadron and group officers. The new replacement crews were coming and going so fast, I finally refused to eat in the combat mess and ate with the ground officers.

"April 24th, my 25th mission. This was the sixth crew I had trained and my second time out with them. They were about ready to go on their own under their pilot, Bob Brown. The target for the day was an airfield and manufacturing plant in a suburb of Berlin, Oberpfaffenhofen.

"We were leading the low squadron that day, with Col. Dale O. Smith leading the group and the wing, which consisted of three heavy bomb groups. The high squadron was led by Bud MacKichan, who was married to a girl from Saginaw, Michigan, where my parents lived. Bud's wife and my mother had become friends.

"Take off was normal; but shortly after we began our climb to altitude, we lost a supercharger on one of the engines and as a result my low squadron began to lag behind the group. Colonel Smith radioed to close it up, but I just couldn't do it while climbing. I thought to myself, once I'm at altitude we'll be alright and I can close up tight. During this period I began to think about aborting the mission, something I had never done as a first pilot. I had had enough of those as a co-pilot. Also, I had five planes flying formation on me and they were all inexperienced pilots with few missions. I probably should have aborted, but I didn't. We finally got to bombing altitude and little by little we were closing in. I could see Paris far below and to the south of us. It was a perfect Spring day, not an enemy fighter in sight and our own escorts of Mustangs and Thunderbolts all around us.

"Suddenly the sky below us was filled with little black puffs. Those innocent-looking puffs were anti-aircraft shells exploding just beneath our group. A few seconds later the Germans found our range and the puffs were all around us. Just then our B-17 lurched and I knew we had been hit. I looked around and the back of the cockpit was on fire. This had happened to me on a previous mission and I had been able to get it out. So, I told Brown to take over and I would go back and try to put out the fire. No luck this time. So, I rang the alarm and told the crew to bale out, grabbed Brown by the arm and said 'let's go.' The bombardier and the navigator already had the forward escape hatch open and were waiting for my signal. A thumbs down did it and the four of us were out and away.

"When we were lectured on how to parachute, three things were stressed. Number one, 'free fall' as long as possible so the enemy fighters can't follow you down and shoot you. Number two 'free fall' so that the ground forces can't follow you down and be there to meet you as you land. Number three, save the rip-cord ring as a souvenir. The first and second I did, the third I didn't. When the chute jerked open, and I thought it never would, it geve me a hell of a jerk. I realized I hadn't tightened my leg straps enough and they were really cutting into me. I would lift one leg at a time to release the pressure which helped, but in the meantime I was swinging back and forth and beginning to get airsick. I couldn't see any other parachutes in the sky no matter where I looked. Still, I did think that Bud MacKichan must have seen what had happened and would be able, through his wife, to tell my family that the plane didn't explode, that he had seen parachutes and that I probably would be okay. That report never got home however. Bud was killed a few minutes after I went down.

"On looking down, I could see a small village in a generally wooded countryside. On the edge of the village was a lone building with lots of people looking up at me. I thought, 'Oh God, the Germans are just waiting for me.' But as I got closer I could see the building was a school house and the people were little kids waving and yelling and there were no Germans in sight. I landed about one hundred yards from the school in a freshly plowed field . . . couldn't have picked a much better place to land. I Tumbled over a couple of times and got to my feet hauling in the chute at the same time. Finally I got it all together and started to run to some woods a couple of hundred yards away. Then I did one of the only really foolish things that I did in the four months I was in occupied France. I just wasn't thinking. After running about one hundred yards. I dropped the chute in the field and kept running. The chute was just too heavy and I kept getting tangled up in the shroud lines. If the Germans had found it, of course, they would have known right where to look for me.

"Upon reaching the edge of the woods, I looked around and the school teacher had sent the kids out to get the chute and they were dragging it back to the school house. By the time the Germans got there in their trucks and on their motorcycles, I was well hidden in the woods and the parachute was well hidden somewhere in the school house. Luck spelled with a capital L.

"Over the years I've returned several times to visit the French people who helped me. When I would return to Faux Fresnay, the little village where I landed, I would always ask about the school teacher. No one seemed to know what happened to her. Then one time on the thirtieth anniversary of my landing, I figured that this was probably my last visit so my wife, Betty, and I decided to have a party at the hotel in Sezanne. We invited all the people in that area who had helped me. The local paper sent a photographer and a reporter and they did a nice story, including a picture. A few weeks later I received a letter from France. It was from the school teacher. She was still subscribing to the Sezanne paper after all these years. It was the first she had heard about my bombardier and me since the 24th of April 1944. I wrote a long letter back and although we have never met, she now at least has my sincere thanks.

"About six that evening, after the Germans had given up the search and after I had buried my flying clothes and, with great reluctance, had included my roommate, Mike Mazer's, leather flight jacket, which I had borrowed when I couldn't find my own, I crawled to the edge of the woods and soon saw a man who was obviously looking for me. Realizing that I had to have help and with the hope that he was not a collaborator, I stood up and waved my arm. He quickly saw me and walked over. I said, 'American pilot', and he held out his hand and said, 'Bon jour, American.' After offering him a cigarette, he sign-languaged to me that I should wait for him at this spot and he pointed to my watch, letting me know that he would return about eleven that night. I soon learned that everybody was always shaking hands in France.

"After a couple of hours, I decided that perhaps this man wasn't as he appeared and that I had better move away some distance so that I would at least have a chance to escape if he came back with the Germans.

"It was just getting dark, and for the first time, I began to feel fear. Every sound spooked me and every shadow began to look like a German. 'What the hell am I doing here?,' I thought. Would I ever see home again? How sad it will be when my parents get the inevitable telegram. Well, at least my brother is probably okay. I didn't know that he had already been wounded in Italy and was even then a prisoner of war. My folks, I learned much later, had decided not to tell me that he had by then been reported missing in action.

"After a few minutes of feeling sorry for myself, I thought about the matters at hand. We had often been instructed, if we were shot down, to head for Spain and that the Spanish would see that we got back to England. The only other alternative was to go to Switzerland, but the Swiss would not send you to England, that being all but impossible from their land-locked country. So, first things first, I would head for Spain. Of course, at that time, I didn't know that the RAF were flying in at night and picking up evaders. I found out much more about that later.

"On moving to a new spot a hundred yards away, for the first time I did some serious praying—for my mother, father, brother and myself. I wondered what Mike Mazer, my roommate, would think when he returned from the three-day armament school he was attending. I remembered the day he had first shown me his new dog tags with his 'new name', Michael McMazer, inscribed on them. With a name like Nathan Mazer he wouldn't have a chance with the Germans if he were shot down. He said that he was damned if the Krauts were going to find out that he was a Heeb. After that, when we would be checking in to a hotel in London, he would register as Michael McMazer and then innocently ask the clerk for directions to the nearest Catholic church. What a guy! But he was still going to be pissed off about the flight jacket now buried about three feet under the ground. Many years later, back in those same French woods, I tried to find the spot where I had buried it. I thought I could go right to it. I couldn't.

"An hour later, I was studying the stars. My old Boy Scout training came in handy. . . saw a few constellations I knew and then, the North Star, which I was to use many nights in the near future.

"It was just about eleven and I heard a voice calling, 'Big Dog,' a nickname I had somehow acquired. It was Dick Rader, my bombardier, a tall, lanky West Virginian, along with the man I had met that day. His name, Dick said, was Charles Vallon and he had found Dick an hour or so earlier, and told Dick that he had a comrade of his nearby. We were sure glad to see each other. Dick had seen some other chutes in the sky, but that was it. Charles took us to the small village of Faux

Fresnay and on to his house. He had no sooner introduced us to his pregnant wife and his pregnant daughter when four men came in and, after shaking hands all around, we were soon communicating with a few words and much sign language. The men told us that they would bring us clothes and that we must get rid of our own and especially our shoes, as they were dead giveaways. The problem was Dick, who is about 6'3" tall, while I am 5'9", more the average Frenchman's size. Anyhow, there was one tall guy, Gaston Varlet, in the village and they soon brought him over and he said, 'I'll give you my wedding clothes.' Gaston and his wife, Bertie, were wonderful people and we have seen them on all our visits back to Faux Fresnay. The pants were a little short, but not bad. As soon as we changed and all our clothes were taken away, someone said 'how about an aperitif,' and out came the L'eau de Vie, the homemade white lightning so common all over France. We could barely get it down, but we had no choice, so we drank it. Sometime later we found another, and much better, use for it. Eventually, we both caught the crabs and then we discovered a real use for this 'water of life'. We rubbed it on ourselves and it put the crabs to sleep for two or three days and when they awakened we would put some more on. What a relief.

"For the next eight days we lived in the woods. We had bales of straw to sleep on, some blankets, and we built a lean-to and even put up a sign, 'Savoy Hotel.' We built the lean-to on the edge of a cool stream where we kept our supply of wine, including champagne, cold and ready to drink. We had both red and white wine, apple cider and beer. How good could it get? The whole village was feeding us. One couple, the Morant Gobins, couldn't have been kinder to us. We saw them many times after the war. We lived the best there that we ever did while in occupied territory. Of course, it was too good to last.

Chuck Yeager was a member of the 357th Fighter Group, Leiston, England on 5th March 1944 when he was shot down by a Focke-Wulf 190. Of his eighth combat mission he wrote: "Free-falling. Flat on my back. Spinning from 16,000 feet. Velocity doubling each second. Hold off. Get below clouds where krauts can't see chute. Yank that cord now, you're dead. Germans strafe guys floating down. Clouds whisk past. French countryside filling horizon. Even so, wait, Goddamn it. Ground rushing up. Occupied territory.

"Two fingers grip chute ring.

"A canister of carbon dioxide hooked to my Mae West bangs close to my head. It's tethered to the dinghy we sit on in the cockpit, and the dinghy, which the CO_2 inflates if we go down in the Channel, flaps in the wind like an enormous doughnut. I unclip the canister and the dinghy; they fall away. Corner of my eye—ground closing in. I Smell the forests and fields below.

"Now.

"I yank the ripcord ring.

"The parachute blossoms, breaking my fall, and I'm rocking gently in the winter sky. Below me, the hills and fields are crawling with Germans. I see the black smoke from my airplane wreckage and sweat the slow ride down. I'm easy target practice from the ground.

"I hear a dogfight raging far above me—the chattering machine-guns and roaring engines of fighter planes spinning across the sky above a dull grey cloud deck. I'm dropping down over southern France on a deceptively peaceful countryside. I work the shroud lines toward a pine forest.

"Trees rush up at me. I reach out and grab on to the top of a twenty-foot pine. I bounce a couple of times on that limber sapling, leaning it over to the ground, just as I did as a kid in West Virginia, when we'd ride pines for miles through the woods. In only seconds, I'm six inches from the ground; I step down, gather in my parachute to use later as a shelter, and limp off into the woods. There's blood on my pant leg, blood on my torn leather gloves, and blood dripping down the front of my flying jacket from my head.

"I treat my wounds in deep brush. There are shrapnel punctures in my feet and hands from the shells that hit around my cockpit; I've got a hole in the lower part of my right calf from a fragment that tore through my fleece-lined boot, and a gash on my forehead from banging against that CO_2 canister when I fell out of my dead airplane. I sprinkle sulfa powder on the leg wound and bandage it, then study a silk map of

Europe that is sewn into our flight suits. I'm about fifty miles
east of Bordeaux, near the town of Angoulême, where our
bombers had blasted a German airdrome five minutes before
I was shot down.

"I study my escape map, trying to figure my best route across the
Pyrenees into Spain. The deep mountain snows should begin melting by late spring; if I can stay clear of the Germans, I might be
able to contact the French underground for help. There would be
no help if these were German woods. I'd wind up a POW, or,
worse, fall into the hands of angry farmers who'd rather use axes
and pitchforks than take prisoners. All of us carry forty-five caliber
automatics; mine is gripped in my right hand.

Even now, in shock from being shot down, cold and scared, I
figure my chances are good for coming out of this alive. I know
how to trap and hunt and live off Mother Nature. Back home, if
we had a job to do, we did it. And my job now is to evade capture
and escape.

"I can ssurvive in these woods for as long as it takes to keep the
damned Germans from finding me and hauling me off to a POW
camp. But whatever happens, for me the war is over. If I make it
over the Pyrenees and manage to get back to England, I'll be sent
home. No more combat—a rule meant to protect the French
underground from pilots they assisted, who might later be shot
down again and tortured by the Gestapo into revealing escape net-
works. So far, none of the guys shot down in my squadron have
been able to make it back.

"Our commanding officer, Capt. Joe Giltner, was shot down on
a strafing run near Antwerp. Joe bailed out, tried to evade the
Germans and get to the coast. But his wounded foot hurt so much
he was forced to hobble. Finally, he sat down, undid his boot, and
discovered the cause of his pain when his shot-off big toe plopped
on the ground. The Germans captured him. Because I was a junior
officer, but a good pilot with exceptional eyes, I flew my first
missions as wingman to the group commander. Col. Henry Spicer,
a daring pilot with bristling mustaches, who loved to dogfight
and could care less about the personal risks. Spicer smoked a big
briar pipe, and on the return home, he always dropped down to
below 12,000 feet, unhooked his oxygen mask, and had himself
a smoke. As his wingman, I dropped down with him right over

Paris. German flak guns began pounding at us. We were practically over the rooftops when tracers flashed by my canopy. Colonel Spicer was later shot down by a burst of white flak near the French coast, after he had descended to light that damned pipe. He bailed out over the Channel, but the Germans picked him up.

"I decide to stay put in the heavy brush until dark. I peek out and see a woodcutter shouldering a heavy ax. I decide to rush him from behind and get that ax, killing him if necessary. I jump him and he drops the ax, almost dead with fright. With eyes the size of quarters, he stares at the pistol I'm waving in his face. He speaks no English, so I talk at him like Tarzan: 'Me American. Need help. Find underground.' He jabbers back in excited French, and if I understand right he tells me he will go get somebody who speaks English. I read his face, which is scared but friendly. He grins and nods when I say I'm an American. Puts a finger to his lips to whisper, 'Boche,' then hurries off into the forest, after signaling to me to stay hidden and wait for him to get back. I keep his ax and watch him run off; then I move across the path into a stand of big trees, wondering if I should take off or wait for him. Can I trust the guy?

"Long before I see them, I hear returning footsteps. Definitely more than one person, but whether they are more than two, I can't tell. It's been more than an hour since that woodcutter took off. I move back into the stand of trees and drop down. My pistol is pointing at the path. I won't get very far if he's brought a squad of German soldiers. I'm burrowed into the wet ground, my heart thudding like a five-hundred-pound bomb as the footsteps stop. My impulse is to turn tail and run, but I check it. Then I hear a voice calling to me in a whisper. 'American, a friend is here. Come out.' I can't see them and it takes all my courage to slowly pick myself up. I'm on the opposite side of the path from where the woodcutter left me. My .45 is aiming at the back of an old man staring into the brush. The woodcutter is with him. Silently, I move forward."

INTERNEES

THE FALL OF 1943 was the nadir in the fortunes of the US Eighth Air Force. In the course of the first and most cruel Schweinfurt mission and three others, 148 aircraft had been shot down. The Fortresses and Liberators, despite their heavy armament, were taking heavy punishment from flak over the target and from fighters all along the route. In some bomb groups, morale was pretty low. Aborted sorties were more common, and the number of crews breaking off from their formations to land in neutral territory, not always with good reason, steadily increased. By the summer of 1944, nearly a thousand of General Eaker's airmen were interned in Sweden, and as many more in Switzerland.

In a summary of information in documents from the US National Archives, USAAF historical repositories, the Swiss Airchives, the Swiss newspapers, Yank August 12, 1945, letters and diaries of internees, Robert A. Long, the president of the Swiss Internees Association, Inc., USA, has provided the following data: The US Army Air Forces suffered heavy losses in the air war over Germany in 1943-45. A number of crippled or malfunctioning aircraft sought to reach Switzerland rather than accepting such grim alternatives as landing, crash-landing or baling out in German-occupied territory and becoming prisoners-of-war, crashing or ditching while trying to make it back to their English bases.

There were two groups of American airmen in Switzerland during the war: EVADEES (evaders) whose aircraft had not made it to the Swiss border when they bailed out over German territory, evaded capture by the Germans and crossed into Switzerland on foot, and INTERNEES whose aircraft crossed over the Swiss border. They then either landed, crash-landed or baled out, landing within the Swiss border.

1,045 American airmen were interned in Switzerland between 1943 and 1945. 167 USAAF aircraft were interned there, of which 96 were salvaged as junk, and 70 were repaired requiring more than 19,000 hours of 1st and 2nd echelon repair work.

In 1944, an American diplomat assigned in Sweden, wrote to the USAAF Command claiming that many American aircraft then in Sweden and in Switzerland were, in fact, undamaged, and alleging cowardice and desertion on the part of the crews. General Carl Spaatz, USAAF, insisted then that USAAF personnel be allowed to examine the American planes and immediately assigned a USAAF Major (an aircraft maintenance supervisor) and a five-man ground crew to go to Switzerland for that purpose. Spaatz thought the charges slanderous. The aircraft were inspected and the inspectors reported that "no USAAF aircraft in Switzerland was there without just cause." The American officer remained in Switzerland, checking each new USAAF aircraft arriving there for the remainder of the war. He remained there well after the war ended, to supervise the work on the repairable US aircraft. His final report does not cite any aircraft in Switzerland as being there without just cause.

On Friday, 13th August 1943, a B-24 bomber named *Death Dealer*, flying from Bengazi in North Africa to bomb a target at Weiner-Neustadt, was crippled by flak and, with two engines out, was unable to cross the Alps for a return to its base. It crash-landed near Wil in eastern Switzerland; the first such Grenzverletzungen (border violation).

When an American airman arrived in Switzerland by aircraft or by parachute in that time, he was quickly surrounded by the local police or the Swiss military, the latter brandishing bayonetted rifles and machine-guns. He was photographed, finger-printed and interrogated. The interrogation varied from brief to lengthy. At Dubendorf, where many were taken for interrogation, they reported that the interview was conducted by a Swiss Major who spoke American English. His mother, he told them, was American and his father Swiss. They were under twenty-four hour armed guard during their entire stay in the country. Initially, many of them were placed in town or city jails. They were transported to small villages high in the Swiss Alps and were assigned to stripped-down hotels there. Some of these hotels had been condemned as unfit for human habitation and were scheduled to be demolished. Others were reasonably habitable. Most were unheated, and one had to dress as if outside even when in the building. There was no hot water for bathing or shaving, and the water in the wash bowls would often freeze. When the toilets froze, a bucket was brought in. Soap and toilet paper were rarely provided.

There were more than 104,000 refugees and more than 1,000 American internees in Switzerland in 1944 when all food imports were halted. The country was able to produce only about 50% of its food requirement and was in a difficult situation. In the hotels where the internees were being kept, much of the food was poor and all of it was monotonous and meagre in quantity. A typical daily menu would include a rye roll with a spoon of jam, ersatz coffee, tea or cocoa for breakfast; a bowl of watery potato soup and a slice or two of bread for lunch; Rosti potatoes and half a cup of shredded cabbage for dinner. There were five meatless days per week. There were many meatless weeks. Meat, when there was any, was a slice of braunschweiger or blood sausage. In winter months meals were eaten wearing gloves in the frigid buildings.

Some escape from the boredom was available to the internees via musical instruments that were provided by the YMCA, and some bands were formed. Language classes for French and German were offered as well.

There were two Red Cross inspections, one in 1943 and another in 1944. Many of the internees reported that these inspections were "staged", as the food during the inspections was certainly not the usual fare.

Upon arriving in the village that was to be the internee's permanent billet for the duration of the war, he was not permitted out of his hotel building for the first two weeks of his stay. After that, he was allowed to roam the streets of the village within certain limits. He could be shot by guards if he attempted to go beyond the posted limits for internees. After D-Day, the guards were tripled and the machine-gun emplacements doubled. Guards were supposed to call 'Halt!' three times before firing, but internees who were wounded in these circumstances claim that the command 'Halt!' and the firing were simultaneous. There were from one to three bedchecks a night, depending on where an internee was billeted.

Some money was doled out through a Swiss 'chit' system until early in 1945 when the internees were given their pay and their allowances. Many received a sizeable check to settle back pay and allowances, when they returned to the United States at the end of the war.

Paroles were applied for and granted to some internees, allowing them to attend Swiss schools, or work with the International Red Cross, and eleven men were paroled to work in the American Cemetery at Munsingen. The parole permitted the internee to leave the internment site and participate in the activity. If he escaped while on parole, under the terms of the Geneva Convention the United States would be compelled to return him to Switzerland. He would then serve a prison sentence, but not at his former internment site. It is known that one such American was sent back.

Three camps, Adelboden and Wengen (for enlisted men) and Davos (for officers) were established in 1944.

All prisoner escape is risky and hazardous, and attempting escape in the Swiss Alps is even more so. There were people in that situation known as 'coyotes' who would ask from $100 to $800 to assist one in an escape. When the would-be escapee crossed the Swiss border and attempted to meet up with the contact party arranged by the coyote, he was often met by the Nazis instead. It seems probable that these arrangers were collecting fees from the escapers and the Nazis alike.

If one was apprehended by the Swiss while trying to escape, he would be sent to Hunenburg or Straflager Wauwilermoos prison camps. They also had to spend a period of time in city or town jails which were little more than medieval dungeons. The camp at Wauwilermoos was the worst place to be sent, reportedly worse than any Nazi camp. The Kommandant of Wauwilermoos was arrested in August 1945 and had a military trial which lasted for 149 days. He was a Swiss Nazi who had been protected through the war by higher Swiss Nazis. He was accused of embezzling, of being a con-man, and of inhuman treatment of prisoners. His ill-gotten gains had helped him to support four mistresses. He was convicted, sentenced to prison, stripped of his Swiss citizenship and banned from the Army for having disgraced it.

Wauwilermoos and Hunenburg had double rows of 8' barbed wire fencing, which was patrolled by armed guards and vicious dogs on the lighted perimeter each night. The prisoners slept on the ground on a thin layer of straw and received one thin blanket per man.

Sanitary facilities consisted of a single outhouse. The food was horrible and was poured into slop pails and then into tin cups or cans. Every man sent to these places lost a lot of weight, suffered from pyorrhea, dysentery, and had boils and other skin afflictions. The solitary confinement area had no sanitation facilities and one side of the enclosure had a trench latrine that was hosed down once a week. Food was put into a trough from the outside and the men were treated like animals. They were held in these places for weeks incommunicado before a trial was mounted and, if the prisoner made a statement at his trial, the sentence was extended. Minor infractions resulted in internees being sent to the aforementioned dungeons in the towns and cities, where they subsisted for up to three weeks on bread and water only and in conditions of utter filth.

For the internees, repatriation was a possibility, but happened only infrequently until February 1945. These exchanges were for Germans and at a ration of two Germans for one American.

61 American internees died before or during their stay in the custody of the Swiss, and were buried in the American Cemetery at Munsingen. In 1948, the US State and Defense Departments ruled that the Munsingen Cemetary would no longer be maintained as an American cemetery, and the internees were disinterred, many of them being returned to the United States at their families' requests. The remainder were reburied at Epinal, France.

From the Geneva Convention relative to the treatment of prisoners of war: Traditional international law imposed obligations on neutrals to exclude combatants from their territory and to intern them if they in fact entered neutral territory during the course of a conflict. If required to be interned under international law, such persons must generally at a minimum receive the benefits of GPW treatment. Special provisions are made for the sick and wounded, including those who are brought by medical aircraft. However, escaped PWs are generally not interned. Regulations for the treatment of internees, contained in Articles 79-135, are similar in many respects to GPW provisions protecting PWs. They embrace such matters as places of internment, food and clothing, hygiene and medical attention, religious, intellectual, physical activities, personal property and financial resources, administration and discipline, relations with the exterior, penal and disciplinary sanctions, transfers of internees, deaths and release and repatriation. Under Article 35, a protected person (enemy alien) who has been denied permission to leave the jurisdiction may have such denial reconsidered by an appropriate court or administrative board designated for that purpose by the detaining power. A similar right is provided by Article 43 for protected persons interned or placed in assigned residence in a party's home territory. Article 78 likewise provides that persons placed in internment or assigned residence in the occupied territory are entitled to a review or reconsideration by a 'competent body' and the administrative boards and the competent bodies contemplated by the three Articles to reconsider decisions in these cases may be created with advisory functions only, leaving the final decision to a high official or officer of the government.

The internment provisions of the Geneva Convention do not require a belligerent government to hold a hearing before it interns an alien enemy in time of crisis. However, they do require that internment be used with discrimination, common sense and in accordance with certain restrictions, e.g., that opportunities for reconsideration must be provided as a safeguard against mistakes.

HOW I GOT THROUGH IT

THE 376TH BOMB GROUP'S B-24s of the 15th US Air Force were based near Naples in Italy. On Christmas Day 1944, their mission was to attack a target in Hall, on the mountainous border between Austria and Germany. The airplane in which Frank Kautzmann was flying as bombardier was hit by flak on the run-in to the aiming point, and burst into flames. The crew baled out safely, all were captured and imprisoned in various German camps until they were released by General Patton's soldiers in May 1945. In his excellent chronicle, MIA World War II, of those five months in captivity, Kautzmann gives an insight into the sort of thoughts that kept him going. "I have to have faith in FDR and the military strategists who are in control of how this war will end. And this war will end. I can see it in the eyes of the guards when our planes fly overhead. They are frightened, angry, confused. They sense there is no longer a center to the great Nazi war machine. Their false god seems to have become obvious, even to them."

"The first compound at Barth," recalls Don Ackerson, "was mostly British. There was a recreation hall with a stage and plays and musicals were put on. There were also boxing matches and other sports. The treatment at this time was good—strict, but fair."

By the time Bobby Stark had joined the Third Reich's guests at Stalag Luft III in June 1943, the POWs' techniques of producing alcohol had passed, as he recorded, the experimental stage. Dried fruit from US Red Cross parcels, with water and a modicum of yeast, having been allowed to ferment in a forty-gallon barrel, was passed to two Czech officers who, in return for a fifth share of the product, continued the process in a home-made still. The resulting beverage, with the addition of powdered lemonade—an American contribution—was both palatable and potent, and preservation in a bottle with a few dried apricots augmented its effects. It as to the credit of the German officers and guards that, at Christmas, they turned a blind eye to the condition of the prisoners.

Luther Cox, remembering Sagan: "Activities in the camp were varied. The most important of all, holding top priority were the 'X' activities (escape). For others who preferred to occupy their minds along different channels, there were a few books and also some classes in the sciences and languages. These were usually conducted by men, who before the war, were leaders in education or other professions. They were brilliant men, many had degrees. Several could fluently write, read and speak half a dozen different languages. These men shared their wealth of information by giving lectures to those who were interested. Many of the older Kriegies who had been down since Dunkirk, have received packages from home and book parcels from the YMCA.

At this stage of the war when there were so few POWs, there was no German limit on how many parcels they could get. This was changed to one parcel a month starting in 1943 around June. Those who were fortunate enough to get educational books shared them with their fellow Kriegies. However, escape activities took absolute top precedence. Never, at any time, did these ever cease. They were in operation day and night, around the calendar. Little groups of Kriegies could always be found working tirelessly on escape plans and activities to support them.

In another corner of the camp there is a church. It is fenced off from the rest of the camp by rows of barbed wire. We are only allowed to enter it for worship on Sundays. A British Padre resides here. The building is never heated so on Sunday you wear everything you can get on when you attend church.

Those attending usually gather in small, very close little groups in order to get the benefits of each others body heat. As we sing, our breath condenses into thin wispy streams, vividly illustrating only too plainly the extremely cold temperatures and the damp atmosphere of the church. Attendance is usually very good, for a POW has much to be thankful for, God has spared his life! To anyone else it may not be fully understood that indeed this is a blessing. To me it is, for life is very precious even though at times we are forced to live like animals, caged up and treated as such. I do not ever question God in this respect, although there have been many times over the years that I have wondered, 'Why me, God?' There were so many good men in my crew of ten and here we are, just Gus and myself. It had to be the Hand of God that led that small Arab fishing boat to us, floating out there in the vastness of the Mediterranean Sea. There is no doubt in my mind that for some reason, God spared me that fateful day out of a crew our aircraft, *Double Trouble*."

1st Lt. George A. Behling, Jr. flew a P-51 Mustang, *Chi-Lassie*, with the 357th Fighter Group out of Leiston, England. On 14th January 1945, Behling took off on his 42nd mission to Germany. He was downed near Berlin, captured by German soldiers and then taken to Stalag Luft III: "After about a month, several things happened that ameliorated our conditions considerably. First, and probably most importantly, we received the Red Cross parcels. Never underestimate the Red Cross. They not only furnished the parcels, but actually got them distributed to us. Each parcel contained spam, cheese, crackers, jam, coffee, 5 packs of cigarettes and other things that skip my mind. We each got a parcel every week and it helped so much. Some of the bigger men had lost a lot of weight. Again, I was lucky, only losing 10 pounds.

"The Red Cross parcels induced bartering and one of the men actually built up a store where you could trade for whatever you wanted. He built up his inventory by requiring a premium for every item—a true entrepreneur.

"Some of the men made bets that they could finish an entire parcel in 24 hours. None of them won, always being stopped by the cigarettes or coffee, and one man had a quarter of a jar of powdered coffee left, a half hour to go and had to give up. His throat was so sore he couldn't swallow.

"There was no shortage of cigarettes. To pass the time and alleviate my hunger I started to smoke for the first time in my life. This developed habit plagued me for the next 22 years.

"The second favorable happening was the weather. About early March it started to moderate. We had sunny days and could get outside to warm our chilled bones. We finally even played baseball. It was food and warmth—a double-barreled simple combination of basic need that most of us had never before given serious thought.

"I made several friends, one a second lieutenant infrantry officer who told me the only way to get off 'the line' was to get killed, wounded or captured. He was weary and said that most of his comrades hoped for a minor wound, the lesser of the evils, that would send them back from the lines. Because of their experience they had learned that their superiors' talk and promise of rotation was only a dream.

"Another friend, George Ross, a bomber copilot from California, told me how he had romanced girls before the war by telling them he was in the movies. He would mention an obscure scene in a popular movie and tell them he was that actor. Naturally, the girls wouldn't remember the scene, even though they'd seen the movie, and he being a Tom Selleck type, they'd gobble up the bait. I mention this now because our basic hunger and warmth requirements being off zero, we spent our hours talking of home, food and, of course, women."

Larry Hewin, a B-24 Liberator pilot with the 93rd Bomb Group, Hardwick, England, was downed in Holland on 18th September 1944, badly wounded and made a prisoner of the Nazis. "After the crash-landing," he remembered, "the Germans soon arrived and hauled us away on a wagon to a building, possibly a country schoolhouse, that they were utilizing as a field hospital. If this account seems somewhat fuzzy at this point, it is possibly because when the first German medic I encountered asked if I had had any morphine, I lied and said no, so he administered some more. I can honestly say I was feeling no pain at the time . . .

"Oflag 64 was an old and well-established camp. The American staff was organized along the lines of a typical regiment or battalion. The German guard then took me inside the barbed wire and turned me over to the American camp adjutant, who explained something of the setup to me.

"Still not able to walk upright, I was once again put in the camp hospital. The hospital was well-staffed with doctors and had better medical supplies than elsewhere due to its longer history. The food in the hospital was as good as a POW is ever likely to get, better than outside the hospital in the same camp. And it was quite warm, an attribute sincerely appreciated since we were now well into winter.

"Before this time, the places I had been had had few amenities. I was pleased to find Oflag 64 had a library, a camp newspaper, and other niceties. For example, there was a young officer who came regularly to the hospital ward in the evenings with a record player and classical records. He would lecture on the music and the composer and play the compositions.

"I had some very congenial companions in the hospital. In the bed right next to me was Wright Bryan, a civilian war correspondent for the *Atlanta Constitution*, a Clemson graduate, and an extremely intelligent and charming fellow. Wright had become very friendly with a Catholic priest who came over nearly every evening for conversation and sometimes chess. They usually included me in their lively discussions, which I enjoyed since both of them had considerably more experience and wisdom than I.

"But there were also some less fortunate souls. We had a West Point Lt. Col. of Infantry who was in our ward for jaundice. His more serious problem was psychological. He had trained for battle at West Point, then for much of the war had to train others, all the while pleading for a combat command. Finally, he had been assigned one and committed to combat. Almost immediately, his unit had been overrun by a German attack, defeated, and the Germans captured him. The effect on him was devastating; his entire waking day was devoted to fretting about his perceived failure and his desire to escape, and get another command, and redeem himself in his own eyes.

"I first became aware of the problem when he found out that I was a pilot and approached me. His proposition was that he was sure that there was a German fighter base maybe fifty or sixty miles away. He and I should escape, steal a fighter plane, and fly westward to the Allied zone.

"I tried to explain that I could not at that time even walk upright, I was not a fighter pilot, couldn't read German, and we would probably have trouble even getting the engine started. The fighters were single-place aircraft, and even if we overcame all that, it would be doubtful that the fuel would be sufficient to make the trip, and it was doubtful that we, given our respective medical conditions, could manage the escape from Oflag 64. Also it was most unlikely that the Escape Committee who controlled all escape efforts would approve. I felt extremely sorry for him as did the others but nothing we said seemed to help.

"There were two other pilots at Oflag 64 who had been sent there by mistake and had just stayed because it was an established and, as camps went, not as bad as some. The Germans apparently did not know they were pilots and the pilots didn't care to tell them.

They too had been asked by the Lt. Col. to escape and steal a plane.

"Oflag 64 did its best to make Christmas of '44 a real Christmas. There were decorations, caroling, modest gifts and special meals created from carefully hoarded supplies. We also were cheered by the rate of advance of the Russians on the eastern front—they were getting close enough that it was becoming clear it would not be much longer, if there were no reverses, before the Germans would have to do something about us. The concern, however, was what? We always wondered if they would they try to fight? Surrender? Evacuate? If so, how?

"Shortly after Christmas, I was released from the hospital and was assigned to regular barracks. I could walk upright but not well due to the severed muscles, impaired circulation and the atrophy of muscles that had occurred over several months without exercise. The doctors prescribed a program of gradually increasing walks around the camp area.

"Barracks life was an abrupt change from the hospital. We were now in the middle of the Polish winter, the barracks had almost no heat, and everyone was chilled nearly all of the time. Our conversation was usually brief and desultory since our energy levels were low.

"One day a guard came in and called out, 'Lt. Hewin!' When I replied he said with some indignation, 'You should not be here!' 'Fine,' I said, 'When am I going home?' 'Nein, nein, you are a pilot and you must go to the Stalag Luft!' Well, I had tried to tell them that for several months and it had finally penetrated. He said they would make arrangements and that I should be prepared to go shortly.

"The trip to Sagan, Stalag Luft 3, was again by rail coach, and I was accompanied by two guards who had nothing to distinguish themselves except their indifference.

"I was assigned to a barracks and a specific room within that barracks. The room's occupants (I think there were eight or nine) functioned as a communal group in almost every sense of the word. All Red Cross parcels and German issue food were pooled, and the group ate meals prepared by two members elected as cooks by the common consent of the group. Some others of us shared the more menial chores such as the clean-up, while yet others were specialists.

"One such specialist was our group's trader. Each day he would set out whatever we might have in relative surplus, whether it be cigarettes or canned milk or whatever, to trade for whatever we needed or wanted most. Sometimes he engaged in speculative trading—simply trading for ultimate profit. Everything had a price in cigarettes, that being a common base for all barter. He would sometimes set out with a number of packs of cigarettes in the morning, trade all day and have a nice profit in cigarettes by the evening, having traded a half-dozen or more other commodities during the day. He was exceptionally good at it and we all profited from his operations.

"I had luckily fallen into a relatively prosperous group. Perhaps part of the reason for the prosperity was that some of the Kriegies had been in quite a while, the most senior being a British Flight Officer who had then been in nearly 4 years. They were also a well ordered and congenial group.

"I liked the way things were organized. Breakfast was a lean meal, but the cooks handed out the black bread toast with butter and jam, along with coffee or tea to the others while they were still in their bunks if that was the way they wanted it. Lunch was also a relatively light offering, but we ate it all together at the table. The light breakfast and lunch was made more palatable by the knowledge that the evening meal would be a treat every day. The philosophy was to save up and have that one really good meal each day, and it worked. The trader had contacts among diverse nationalities and traded for things from their private parcels—lentils from Indians, garlic from the French, etc. The two alternating cooks added to our welfare by competing with each other in creativeness.

"The BBC was provided daily from the covertly operated radio, and there seemed to be news from other unidentified sources as well. For example, I had not been there long when we heard that Oflag 64, the camp I had recently left, was being evacuated—the prisoners were being marched west as the Russians advanced on the Eastern front."

FORCED MARCH

IT SELDOM TOOK the POWs long to set up their own intelligence and surveillance systems within the confines of the camp. They had their hidden radios, their coded correspondence with MI9 in London, and information they extracted from members of the staff by the subtle exercise of bribery and blackmail. By the end of January 1945, all at Sagan and its satellite, Belaria, to which Eric Lapham and his mess-mates had been transferred, knew that the Red Army was drawing ever nearer from the east, and were convinced that they would soon be moving in the opposite direction. The ground was covered with a foot of hard-packed snow and, as navigator Lapham recorded, "men overcame their reluctance to break up precious furniture or valued bed-boards, and a whole range of sledges [sleds] were assembled."

The march from Sagan commenced in the early morning of Sunday, 28th January, and for many days the 10,000 marchers received no rations from their captors; they survived on the contents of their Red Cross parcels and on what they could scavenge from the land. They moved in six long columns at a rate of some twenty kilometres a day, spending most of the bone-chilling nights in whatever shelter could be found en route—in barns and cattle sheds, schoolrooms and village halls. One group spent a night in the warmth of a glass works, where they were able to wash their bodies and dry their sodden clothes.

As the march went on, the relationship between the guards and the prisoners underwent a subtle change, as is liable to happen when adversity is shared. Increasingly their guards ignored the order which banned communication with the civil population. Roadside bartering became a common practice—cigarettes for barley, chocolate for bread—and plain theft was not unknown. A goose disappeared from an Oberleutnant's car, and the SBO's appeal for its return failed to save the bird or spoil the meal. Next day, a village hausfrau passed by the marching column unaware that the long bread roll protruding from her shopping bag would no longer be there when she arrived at home.

It is a surprising fact that, in whatever circumstances of cold and hardship, of thirst and hunger, of exhaustion and fatigue, it is often the minor indignities which seem most difficult to bear. "A man grows up," Lapham wrote, "to be familiar with less than private urination, and we had got used to 'forty-holers' for defecation, but to squat en masse in the open or under hedges induced a feeling of degradation I never could adjust to."

In his fine book, *Stalag Luft III*, historian Arthur A. Durand describes the final events leading to the dramatic evacuation of the Sagan camp in late January 1945: "January 27—the prisoners were not to be moved.

"That evening the order was countermanded. About seven o'clock the Germans announced that the camp would be evacuated. The prisoners in South Compound were enjoying the play *You Can't Take It With You* when Colonel Goodrich walked onto the stage and reportedly proclaimed, 'The goons have just come and given us thirty minutes to be at the front gate.'

"There was a mad rush, then much delay and confusion. Some prisoners felt that stalling might allow the Russians to overtake the columns fairly close to camp; others simply had a lot to do just before their departure. Bedrolls had to be repacked to accommodate available food. The men cleaned out cupboards and quickly 'bashed' what could not be carried. They tried to consume as much nutritional food as possible. Approximately five hundred prisoners were too sick to be moved, and a few medical personnel, clergymen and healthy prisoners also remained to help care for them. These men received little assistance from the Germans, but managed to find plenty to eat and drink by scrounging through the various compounds.Finally, on February 6, 1945, they too were removed from the camp, placed inside boxcars, and taken westward to a camp outside Nuremberg where, on February 10, they rejoined the prisoners from West Compound, who had arrived shortly before. With the departure of the sick and wounded, Stalag Luft III ceased to exist as a Luftwaffe prisoner of war camp. What happened to the facilities is not known. At least one prisoner returned to the scene immediately after the war in an effort to locate certain documents . . . the camp was still standing, but he could not find what he sought. At some later date the camp was torn down. Today all one sees at the site is an open field with a monument built by the Polish government in memory of the men who died in the complex of prisoner of war camps in the vicinity of Sagan."

A thaw set in on Friday, 2nd February, and the sledges were abandoned. Humping their precious belongings, the prisoners marched on. Some sat down by the roadside, where they promptly fell asleep, and had to be aroused and spurred on by their friends. On 3rd February, they reached the town of Spremberg and, in an empty Panzer Corps depot, were given mugs of steaming soup—the only hot sustenance provided by the Germans during the four days of the march. In the evening the group from Belaria were loaded into cattle trucks, in which they waited for seven hours, taking it in turn to lie down and stand up, before beginning the halting sixteen-hour journey on to their destination at Stalag IIIa, Luckenwalde, some thirty miles south-west of Berlin. There, after three hours of standing in the drizzle while appells were attempted, the weary POWs were searched, deloused and showered. At six o'clock the next morning, they entered the barracks blocks, three hundred men to each. "I slept on a table," Lapham recalled, "feeling slightly ill and horribly depressed."

Meanwhile, the column from east compound, also in cattle trucks, was traveling through Halle, Hannover and Bremen to the naval POW camp at Marlag-Milag Nord, south-west of Hamburg. "The buildings were damp," wrote Bobby Stark, "and there was no sanitation. There weren't enough beds and men slept on the floor. Bedbugs bit one on the neck and the wrists. However, we didn't mind, because almost every day large forces of American and RAF heavy bombers passed overhead on their way to Hamburg and other targets. It was a delight to hear the bombs exploding on Bremen." By early April the British Army was also getting close, and the march was on again, this time north-east, the destination Lubeck.

Passing through a village, Stark and two mess-mates traded a bar of chocolate for an ancient bicycle (minus tyres), which collapsed the next day beneath the weight of their luggage. Next day's acquisition—half a bar of chocolate for a vintage model pram—proved a better buy. From there on, their progress is described by excerpts from Stark's diary:

APRIL 12TH. As there was no water or wood available to us, we organized foraging parties into every village within a five mile radius. They returned with bales of straw for bedding, eggs, and anything else the farmers would part with. We now appear to be much fitter than the guards, who have lost effective control of the march.

APRIL 13TH. We spent the day resting so that our guards might recover. Ron, Pete and I walk into the town. Civilians very friendly. We buy bread, eggs and potatoes for a few cigarettes.

APRIL 14TH. On road with our pram. Weather fine and very hot. Much air activity by RAF Mosquitos.

APRIL 15TH. Wind moves SE. Cloudy and cold. Most of our walk is through fruit farming country, now covered in blossoms. At 1500 hours we reach the river Elbe.

APRIL 16TH. We cross the river in the 'Franz Schubert' ferry and spend another night in the open.

APRIL 17TH. By 0900 hours everyone has had breakfast and we push our pram to Pinesburg. We stop to examine a bird's nest built partly from RAF 'window'. We pass 1,700 Belgian officers who have been prisoners for five years. The countryside is very like England. We build a shelter with tree branches and enjoy a fine night under cover.

APRIL 18TH. A rest day—no marching. John and Pete see a pheasant and finally kill it with a stick. Some of our friends complain that it isn't cricket to kill, let alone eat, a pheasant out of season.

APRIL 19TH. The march goes well, through wild and wooded country. The road becomes a single track through a field and one wheel of our pram gives us anxious moments. A signpost reads 54 Km to Lubeck.

APRIL 20TH. At 1130 hours we stop for ten minutes—the march is on the Hamburg-Lubeck road.

APRIL 21ST. Raining very hard. 'Wings' rushes off and finds us a barn. We move in with our kit. The goons have no control and the boys find their own billets all over the village—every house has a POW. At 1300 hours I am invited to listen to the BBC news. It is a great thrill to hear it direct from London for the first time in two years. The advance of the 21st Army is going well and it might not be long before they reach our part of Germany. Our pram is in need of repair. We salvage what we can and spend the day making a new wagon.

APRIL 22ND. The countryside is very pretty and there is little sign of war. If it wasn't that there are 2,000 of us on the road one could imagine we were out for a Sunday walk. But in Bad Oldesloe the local police chief is very hostile and pushes us off the footpaths— the cobbled streets are bad for our wagon. At 1620 hours we are allowed in a farm building and make our beds in a concrete sty. The farmer is very co-operative and his animals do not seem to mind sharing their bedroom with us.

APRIL 23RD. Soon after mid-day we cross the Hamburg-Lubeck autobahn. Not a sign of traffic—well done RAF.

APRIL 24TH. All kinds of rumours. We hear Lubeck is crowded, barracks full of lice, very little food. The RAF bomb a target to the SW about 12 miles away. Rumour that Bad Oldesloe is hit. I hope that unpleasant chief of police is on the receiving end. After lunch Pete and I walk over the farm. We talk to a very frightened old lady whose husband has been shot by the SS. On return Pete catches a grass snake—I watch from a safe distance.

APRIL 25TH. Much air activity during the night. RAF Tempests shooting up aerodromes etc. during the morning. Our Luftwaffe guards are posted elsewhere and we entertain our new Lager officer to tea. Later his mistress returns with a bottle of wine.

APRIL 26TH. News after breakfast that we will move to other farms tomorrow. After an inspection, the SBO has flatly refused to accept the barracks in Lubeck."

For those 2,000 men, the long march was over. They spent a week in some barns and haylofts on a great estate, walking in the beech woods and by the gleaming lakes; they received a load of 7,000 Red Cross parcels, which the joy of the moment prompted them to share with the Polish and Russian prisoners who laboured on the farms and the German soldiers who lay wounded in a house on the estate. On 5th May, British Army lorries took them to an airfield beside the river Weser, and Dakota transports flew them on to Melsbroek near Brussels. "On arrival," Stark recorded, "we hear excellent news—Bomber Harris has ordered a fleet of Lancasters to fly his aircrew ex-prisoners home."

For five weeks at Luckenwalde, meanwhile, Lapham and his companions had lived in chaotic conditions of squalor and hunger, and in accommodation which made their hut at Sagan seem palatial by comparison. Things only improved when the POWs themselves contrived to bring some sort of order to the scene. The few Red Cross parcels which began to filter through were scrupulously rationed (a fifth to each man once a week), black markets were discouraged, and plans were made for the running of the camp in the event of a total breakdown of the German administration.

"By mid-day on April 21st," Lapham wrote, "there were signs of desertion. The sentry boxes appeared to be unmanned, and then the other external wire guards disappeared. The last German I saw on duty was the little Volksturmer on the gate between our compound and the sports/appell field that was always kept locked. A tall, moustached POW walked slowly towards him, halted and thrust out a hand, palm up. The little guard looked frantically about him, at the empty towers and the unguarded wire, before taking the key which hung about his neck and placing it in our colleague's palm. Then, rifle at the trail, he scuttled away as though the hounds of hell were after him."

During Bob Braham's ten months in German hands, he and his fellow POWs were on the march twice. While the Americans from Sagan's north compound travelled some two hundred miles north-west to a camp site near Berlin, the British contingent moved on, as has been told, two hundred miles westward, sometimes in cattle trucks, sometimes on foot, to Marlag-Milag Nord. The weather was bitterly cold, and most men suffered from frostbite. On the second move, in April, the destination was Denmark, where the German Army was hoping to establish a front, but, on 2nd May, the British 11th Armoured Division intervened, the long march was over and the prisoners were free.

John Hurd and his group were on the road for eighteen days, walking for two, resting on the third, and sleeping in barns or self-made shelters by the road. They subsisted on American, British and French food parcels carried by their guards, with a daily bowl of soup and a stolen chicken now and then. Hurd ran out of paper for his diary on the seventh day, but he recalled what happened when the long trek ended. "On May 2nd an American jeep with a Captain and a driver came to where we had set up camp on the south bank of the Inn river. The Captain talked to our leaders and the Germans and then left. We were no longer POWs. That night I ate a couple of eggs and got a little sick. I guess they weren't too fresh. The next morning Army trucks brought us some chow. On May 7th we were trucked to an airfield in Bavaria. I was flown by C-47 into France and then trucked to Camp Lucky Strike. I came out of the experience in good shape, but a little underweight."

In his book, *Stalag Luft III*, Bob Neary described the plight of the prisoners during the January 1945 evacuation from the Sagan camp: "There can be no doubt that the ten thousand or more despairing men of Luft III, who 'hit the road' that momentous night as hope sounded from the east, will forever remember the tortuous trek that followed in the ever-increasing fury of the blizzard. Snow fell for four days in near-zero temperatures. Ill-fitting packs, blisters, frozen feet and hands, and sickness all contributed to the misery of the marchers groping their way to some undisclosed destination beyond the reach of encroaching Russian armies. There were seemingly endless hours of marching with occasional rest periods and less frequent stops in barns along the way for much-needed sleep.

"Six days and sixty-two miles from Sagan, a part of the miles-long line entrained at Spremberg for Nuernberg. Others went on to Moosburg, near Munich. The ill-famed French forty-and-eight box cars were employed for transportation and were for the next two days the source of much misery for the occupants, who were packed fifty men and a guard to each car.

"Luft III [POWs] remained at Nuernberg for two months, memorable for its large-scale air raids, lice, bedbugs, fleas and food shortage. The aptly named 'green death' soup, a sickening concoction of ill-tasting worm-ridden dehydrated vegetables, and the 'gray death,' a flat, insipid flour soup the consistency of water . . . This diet, supplemented with German black bread, notorious for its five pound weight, and a few potatoes, caused misery anew as diarrhea and dysentery ran rampant through the march-weary kriegies.

"A secondary hardship of the camp was the prevalence of fleas, bedbugs and lice that manifested themselves at night. Their bites covered every exposed part of the body, including the nose and eyelids. The Germans provided no repellent to combat them."

Bob Doherty wrote a number of poems about his POW experience including the following on his forced march from Heydekrug:

OK, God, don't make me bawl / I know war's war, but this takes all. Who could ever be so vile / To make a cripple trot a mile Handcuffed to a man who's blind / So he won't be left behind?

Who could ever be so vile / To prod with bayonets the while / And threaten any rebel sound / With fury of Alsatian hounds? / Who could ever be so cruel? / Kids who ought to be in school. / Brats who take their sport of us / As we make our exodus / From one plateau of Dante's Hell / To this new Silesian cell.

These blue-eyed blondes, so clean and neat / Lunge with sticks and trip our feet.
—from The Evacuation of Heydekrug

Those young girls in prison are stuck-up or something. / They just don't respond to our whistle and shout. / Maybe they figure they're worse off than we are / Because they're inside while we are without.

But we're passing through on a forced march to Nowhere. / Though bound to end up in a Compound once more. / And, Christ, we are straining our last sense of humor / Which shouldn't be wasted on them to ignore.

The young girls in prison begin clucking forward. / Like mangy old chickens, they step in a flock. / Their noses are beakish, we've ruffled their feathers / Their eyes are unblinking and hollow from shock.

These young girls in prison are very macabre. / They perch in sack-dresses without any shoes. / They reach through the fences and beg us in silence / We see the tattoos which declare they are Jews.

These young girls in prison are maybe Cro-magnons, / For maybe we've walked through dimensions of Time. / Or maybe we're dreaming in mass-type hypnosis / And, really, they're beauties and all in their prime.

The SS is screaming that break-time is over. / The Dobermans bark and the bayonets gleam. / The sign on the vorlager says this is Dachau, The young girls are waiving as if in a dream.
–The Young Girls in Prison, April 1945

Frank Madrid was a ball turret gunner with the 100th Bomb Group at Thorpe Abbotts, England. He recalled his four-month march from Gross Tychow: "The Germans herded us Americans together and began marching us in circles. We marched for four months across northern Germany. And as our troops got closer, we marched in smaller circles.

"The Germans didn't feed us anything. We had to scrounge potatoes and cabbages from farmers.

"Dysentery was rampant. Men who were too weak to march were sent to the back of the line. There was a big truck carrying the sick men. When a man was put on the truck, he'd ride there for a day or two, and then we never saw him again.

"Around May 1, we heard artillery fire. It was the Allied troops. We spent the night in a barn. Artillery shook the barn. The Germans came and told us we would be switching places soon. They would become the prisoners. They wanted to be captured by the Americans. They knew the Russians would kill them. Even the Russian prisoners we knew were mean.

"Early the next morning, the leader of our group left the barn with a white bedsheet. He returned with an English general, who told us we were safe at last.

"They took us to Brussels. We hadn't bathed in five months. They deloused us. I had a long, hot shower—the best shower of my life.

"We didn't get any good, solid meals until we got to Le Havre, France. The doctors didn't want us gorging ourselves all at once. Finally, I went to a restaurant in Le Havre and had a big, juicy steak with onions and mushrooms."

"I think about the men who didn't come back. I especially remember the right waist gunner. His name was Baumgarten. He was from New York City, a little guy, real easy-going.

I think about Baumgarten and wonder about his family and if they remember him on Memorial Day."

THE LAST DAYS

ERIC LAPHAM NOTED HIS MEMORIES of the last days at Stalag Luft IIIa, Luckenwalde, when the guards had left their posts and the fire-fights between the advancing Red Army and the retreating Wehrmacht were raging all around them. "There was the excitement of traversing a still-warm battlefield, strewn with the rubbish of war and animal carcasses. When we visited the town, and you could almost smell the fear . . . we caught glimpses of women and girls, cowering behind shutters. We had heard stories of rape from army POWs, shocked into returning to the camp from the cosy billets they had found outside. We learned of the crudeness and childlike simplicity of the Russian soldiers, most of whom were armed with automatic weapons. We kept a low profile in those early days. Later, in what had been the local Hitler Youth HQ, we bumped into two Russians who both spoke English. We were very sensitive about the Anglo-American halt on the Elbe, and asked them in a casual way where they thought their own advance would stop. We were rather shattered when they said the English Channel."

From the diary of John Hurd, ball turret gunner, 401st Bomb Group, US Eighth Air Force, who was shot down 11th April 1944:

MARCH 9TH. [1945] Barley ration has been cut 28% and spuds 15%. There are enough food parcels for a couple more issues and they are being given out one for two men per week. There is good news from the fighting fronts. Maybe we won't be here much longer.

MARCH 21ST. First day of spring. Many American bombers and fighters were over. They made contrails in all directions, filling the sky everywhere. Boiled spuds for dinner and vegetable soup for supper. News from all fronts is very good.

MARCH 30TH. Barley soup for dinner. The people back home wouldn't feed their hogs this soup, but I am hungry so it's good. Jerry has searched the barracks. The Russians have crossed the Austrian frontier.

APRIL 6TH. Received orders about marching out in a day or two. Our destination is a place eighty kilometers west of here. Received one sixth of a loaf of bread today.

APRIL 7TH. We will be marching out tomorrow. The Germans are allowing extensive trading between other nationalities and us Americans. This camp is really in a mess.

The end of confinement at Sagan was recalled by George Behling: "The days dragged on. Our estimate of the end of the war lengthened. One morning in early April we heard the sound of cannon fire in the distance to the East. Each day it drew nearer. Our leaders set up a plan to take over the camp to preserve order and protect our meagre food supply. About two weeks later we arose and couldn't see a German anywhere. The guards had left. We immediately put our plan into operation. It was a good thought because we did have to ward off other prisoners that attempted to raid the larder.

"The next day about noon a Russian tank column rumbled up to our front gate. What a sight—the tanks were interspersed with an assortment of other vehicles including horse-drawn carts filled with hay, and Russian soldiers, men and women, carrying rifles and a loaf of bread under their arms. They were a solemn, intent group obviously battle and travel-weary, observing us unemotionally. To me they looked like Santa Claus arriving with a sleigh full of goodies.

"The Russians took over command of the camp and we learned that they had joined with the Americans 10 miles to the West. Our leaders negotiated for our return to the American lines but the Russians said they had no trucks to spare. They wouldn't let us walk because they said it was too dangerous considering they were still mopping up.

"The upshot was that they would send us back to Moscow for processing and then home South from the Black Sea. Each morning our numbers dwindled as more and more of us sneaked out at night to find our own way back to the American lines. The Russians didn't tolerate this and set up a guard around the camp.

"The Russian Commandant was a sight to see strolling around with a young German girl five paces behind like a puppy dog.

Every evening scores of German women would flock to the front gate asking to spend the night with them. When we asked what was wrong with the Russians they said 'nothing,' but apparently the Russians would leave them alone if they were seen with an American. Otherwise a parade of Russians would traipse through their bedroom all night long. We also observed one compound that housed teenage German prisoners. Every morning they were let out to exercise by marching around the barracks. And we got to see the Russian quarters adorned with beautiful colored religious scenes on the walls—where they got or how they made their paints is still a mystery.

"One day my Infantry Lieutenant friend said that there were Americans at the Russian command post negotiating our release and suggested that we take a look. Parked in front of the post was an empty jeep and a half-track with American prisoners milling around. Some of the prisoners had climbed onto the half-track. I didn't hesitate and climbed onto the fender of the jeep; my friend found a spot on the hood. Soon both vehicles were completely covered with men inside and out. And about ten minutes later four American officers left the Russian headquarters headed for the jeep and half-track. They were somber and looked straight ahead, completely ignoring our presence. To our surprise they drove off and through the gate with practically no visibility over the bodies on the hoods.

"I was out of the camp and never found out what happened to my comrades left behind. Simultaneously with our escape the Americans had pulled back to the West bank of the Elbe so we had an approximate sixty-mile trip instead of ten. Along the way we saw columns of captured ragged Germans being marched East. In one group I spotted several of our former guards. Also, we had a flat tire and had to call for repairs. While we were waiting we entered a middle class German home. There were only several very old and very young people present. The Russians had come through and smashed every bit of china and glassware with their gun butts. The occupants were petrified wanting to know when the Americans were coming. My heart was cold— I couldn't muster any sympathy even though I knew their fear was justified."

B-24 navigator Bob Weinberg was a guest of the Germans at Sagan, and made the march to Moosburg. He kept a daily diary of his experiences. Here are some entries from his last days in camp in the spring of 1945:

April 25 Announced agreement not to move POWs. Everybody happy. Bread ration cut to 1/10 loaf. Bread wagon strafed. Goons starting to move out. Plenty of air activity. Can hear artillery fine. Weather good and morale at peak.

April 26 Went for wood walk. Country really beautiful. All waiting for Allies to get here. Expect them any minute. Everything seems too good to be true. Plenty of activity at night. We are just about free men, which is so hard to believe. Seems I've been a Kriegie all of my life.

April 27 Another nice day. I got a shower, first one since the middle of February. Allies took command here at 1500, posted our own guards and most of the goons left—only a skeleton crew left. Over 30,000 Allied prisoners here. Bread ration cut to 1/12 loaf.

April 29 The weather cleared up—a beautiful day. P-51s buzzing the place. Lots of ground fire. At 10 o'clock call to quarters blew. A big battle going on outside the camp. A few bullets whizzed overhead and there were a really scared bunch of Kriegies on the floor of the tent. At 1235, the American flag went up over Moosburg. Tanks, jeeps and armored vehicles came into camp. One of the first tank men in met his brother and they broke down and cried. Boys climbed all over the tanks and got souvenirs—goon helmets, guns, bayonets, etc. Still artillery fire at night. This was a day I never will forget. Col. Good tried to keep them from fighting around here but they refused. SS troops shot 20 of the Wehrmacht guards who stayed to surrender the camp according to the Geneva Convention. Luftwaffe left last night. 14th Division of the Third Army liberated us, along with units of the 7th.

April 30 Artillery flying overhead, but we're free. Ransacking all from the goons. Had fresh eggs.

May 1 Lousy weather—its snowing. Infantry moved in. Got 1/4 loaf of white bread—first I've seen since I was shot down. General Patton was here. Ate three full meals today, first time in nine months. Things very disorganized and everyone sore because we haven't moved out.

From the Geneva Convention relative to the treatment of prisoners of war: Section IV (Articles 58-68) contains a number of rules dealing with financial resources of PWs. The detaining power may fix the maximum amount of money which a PW may have in his possession, and any excess must be credited to his account (Article 58).

CAMP LUCKY STRIKE

TWO STAGING AREAS were established in France for the processing of the recently-liberated POWs for their long trip home. They were designated RAMP (Recovered Allied Military Personnel) camps, and were named Camp Chesterfield and Camp Lucky Strike, and the latter was located near Le Havre. In *Kriegie*, a fine record of his own POW experience, Kenneth Simmons describes his visit to Camp Lucky Strike.

"On Monday morning, May 8, 1945, we again picked up our equipment and lined up on the long runways. Our group was to board the tenth plane.

"All at once the sirens from the control tower started blasting away. Then a voice spoke over the loud-speaker.

" 'Attention, all men! Attention all men! The war has ended! The war in Europe is officially over. The German Armies have signed an unconditional surrender, and the war is officially over.'

" 'The planes approaching the field are American C-47s. They will land and unload. When each plane is ready for takeoff, we will call the number from the tower. You have the number of the plane you are to board. You will carry your belongings and move at once to the gangplank for immediate loading and departure. We ask your full cooperation, as we intend to move several thousand of you out of here today.'

"We started walking to plane number ten where she had parked. The pilot of the plane came forward and introduced himself to each of us. He shook hands, and told us it would be a two-hour flight.

"At Le Havre the trucks pulled out on schedule, and we waved goodbye to the French civilians who had cheered our arrival.

"We drove along a coastal highway that overlooked the English Channel. The weather was warm and the sun gave us a feeling of comfort. Some miles out of Le Havre we saw Camp Lucky Strike, an American army base originally designed like an average base in the United States. It covered several miles of land, and was a city within itself.

"We finally came to a long row of buildings at the end of the base.

"Swanson saw the sign first.

" 'Delousing,' he grumbled. 'Not again. Hell, you would think we had bugs or something.'

"We lined up outside to listen to the first doctor. We didn't know it at the time, but before we left Lucky Strike we were going to see more doctors in two weeks than most of us would see the rest of our lives.

"After we had bathed and powdered, we moved down the hall to the clothing department. You didn't have to worry about size—you were issued a whole wardrobe in about three minutes and moved down the line to the dressing room at the other end of the building.

"On the fourth day we finished our medical examinations, but the processing continued. We were gaining better than a pound a day, and most of us were feeling wonderful. The average Kriegie had lost from thirty-five to forty-five pounds.

"On the fifth day we went through the Records, Intelligence, and Information processing centers. We filled out dozens of forms and answered hundreds of questions for Intelligence.

"For the next few days we spent our time at the officers' club, reading, playing pool, poker, and bridge, listening to good music, and drinking malts between meals. All of us were getting fat as pigs. It was good to be in an American military camp and know that we were going home.

"On Wednesday, May 24 we gathered our belongings for departure to Le Havre. From Le Havre we were to board a hospital ship for the United States. We were all excited because this was the final leg of our long journey home. While we were getting packed, Colonel King came into the barracks and told us goodbye. 'I wanted to tell you about General Vandermann and Colonel Spivey. They escaped across the border into Switzerland, as we were told at Moosburg. They went to Eisenhower's headquarters with the captured German generals and made a full report of our imprisonment, the march of death, and our new locations at Moosburg and Nuremberg. They gave valuable advice about our needs and conditions, and they helped in the preparation of rehabilitation centers such as Camp Lucky Strike. Colonel Spivey is still in Europe. General Vandermann flew to Washington several weeks ago to make a full report about us. He also made special recommendations about our leave, pay, and processing, and discharge when we arrive in the States. I think you will all agree that this camp has been extremely efficient and well-organized. General Vandermann is the man responsible for most of it, and I knew you would want o know. Good luck to each of you, and may you find an abundant life in America.' "

"The camp was called 'Lucky Strike,' wrote Frank Kautzmann, "but I came to learn that the name was something of a misnomer. This place was anything but 'Lucky'. It was one hell of a mess. The whole place seemed to operate at some level just above chaos.

"The most frustrating thing of all was that, here we were, all former prisoners of war who wanted nothing so much as to get home and we were stuck at 'Lucky Strike' because there weren't enough ships to carry us back to the States.

"Well, after a few days of American rations and clean clothes, I decided to go and visit 'Gay Paree.'

"We were called back in a hurry. We didn't have passes. Some things never change—like the military.

" 'Just as well,' I figured. 'I didn't have any money either. What the hell was I going to do in Paris without money? Nothing but feel stupid.'

"The Red Cross came through at Lucky Strike just as it had in Nuremberg. They distributed shaving kits and some personal items that made life a good deal more bearable than it had been in a long time. To the Red Cross and all its personnel then and now, you have my respect, my love and affection, and my gratitude. I salute you.

"As bad as Lucky Strike was, it was worlds above prison camp. For starters, we were free and we didn't have to worry about being shot at some guard's whim. Additionally, there were things at Lucky Strike that reminded us that life was worth living.

"There was a blind pianist at the camp, Alec Templeton. One evening, he put on a concert. I sat there and listened in rapture. 'Music!' I said to myself over and over. 'Wonderful music!' Alec Templeton, with his gift of music and his personal warmth, gave us all hope and courage. He brought a little of what was best about home to us and helped us hang on to whatever slivers of sanity we still had. And he was blind! When I thought of the handicap he had overcome, I knew I would be able to put the bad experiences of the war behind me."

Roger Armstrong recalled his stop at Camp Lucky Strike: "Our physical exam was delayed as the Medical Corps took the men in the poorest condition first. It would be May 30th before I received my examination. When I was finally examined, the doctor found I had gained twenty-three pounds in the 30 days after the Germans abandoned Stalag Luft I.

"Each recovered POW was interrogated by an S-2 Army Air Corps Intelligence Officer. After filling out papers identifying our bomb group, and information about where we were shot down, the next questions had to do with the kind of treatment we received at the hands of the German population and armed forces. He wanted dates, names and places. I mentioned our prison guard at Stalag Luft IV, 'Big Stoop.' The S-2 Officer surprised me by revealing his [Stoop's] real name, which I had never actually known. He then said, 'Big Stoop was found with an axe buried in his skull.'

John Vietor recalled Camp Lucky Strike: "The camp was an embarkation point and processing center. Returning prisoners and combat troops swamped the already overtaxed facilities. There were now 25,000 men at the camp and more were arriving every hour.

"Shipping space Stateside was scarce. Desperate efforts were made to repatriate men on a first come, first served basis but it was an almost impossible job. Efforts were made to keep the restless men satisfied with movies, P-X, volley ball, etc., but they were poor makeshifts for home. Many men waited at Lucky Strike for as long as six weeks before getting a boat. Eisenhower flew in and partially straightened the muddle out by doubling the complement of men for each homeward bound ship.

"Throughout the day I scurried around hoping to wangle myself a high priority on an outgoing ship before the other thousands from camps arrived. After considerable finagling I managed to get assigned to a ship sailing within a week. During the next few days I was issued a uniform, ribbons, given shots and my papers were straightened out. Along with the other ex-prisoners, I was put on a regulated diet to prevent overeating and subsequent sickness.

"Theoretically we were all confined to the camp but it made little difference since matters were so disorganized it was easy to slip away. Many men sick of waiting loaded themselves up with cigarettes and took off for Paris. No money was issued us until sailing orders were given, but cigarettes, at that time, were more valuable than francs.

"While I was waiting I spent the evenings with a French family in a nearby village. I had dinner with them every evening, bringing chocolate and cigarettes and little presents for the children and they in turn always had wine or the strong calvados for me to drink. We sat out in their small garden inhaling the heady fragrance of the Normandy spring, discussing the war and life before the war.

"At long last my orders arrived. Trucks transported us to the waterfront at Le Havre and we stopped at different bars in town. We spent the night on the docks and sailed the next day on a converted Grace Line ship. On the trip back officers were quartered in the hold with the enlisted men and the wounded were given the staterooms. The trip back was uneventful, although the Navy still maintained blackouts and gun practice. They couldn't be certain that all German submarine commanders had surrendered.

"We nostalgically looked forward to seeing the Statue of Liberty and the skyscrapers, but the day before we were to sail into New York harbor, the orders were changed for Boston and we sailed anti-climatically into that staid and dirty port.

"There was a brass band, Red Cross girls with coffee to meet us and a few casual onlookers. We weren't worried about what kind of reception we had. We were home at last."

PERIOD OF ADJUSTMENT

RAF WING COMMANDER Bob Braham: "Living in close contact with thousands of other men under conditions of hardship and degradation made unimportant things achieve monumental proportions. A minor argument could very easily flare up into a vicious exchange or lead at times to blows. In the latter stages of the war, the news we picked up . . . about strikes in munitions plants and industrial unrest added much to our bitterness. To POWs, strikes meant a lengthening of the war and more loneliness for us and our families. The mental marks left by prison days made me a difficult person to live with for a time."

Braham admitted that it took him many years to regain his confidence, and as long before he could offer his family the normal, happy life he wanted them to have. "Many a wife," he wrote, "would have thrown me over as a thoroughly bad type."

Eric Lapham, however, discovered that his experience of imprisonment at Sagan was not entirely unrewarding: "I would not have missed it for anything," he said. "I believe I matured more quickly than many contemporaries, and the two years I spent in Stalag Luft III and Luckenwalde were just as profitable as two years at University in terms of personality and character development."

A crush fracture of the vertebrae he had suffered on landing was not diagnosed until a year after his repatriation. By then, the injury had ossified and surgery was not recommended. The prognosis was, as he recorded, "that I would learn to live with the pain and cease to recognise it except in times of stress or poor health. There were others with injuries that lacked medical follow-up, and I suspect that as legacies of prison camp they have proved more permanent than the other physical and mental stresses."

A month or so before his last combat mission in March 1944, Burt Joseph had visited the Haymarket premises of Burberrys, the great London tailors, to be measured for a jacket. Chancing on the correspondence in his records some 45 years later, and noting the tailors' closing paragraph "Assuring you of our best attention at all times", he put tongue in cheek and wrote to enquire whether he might collect the garment on a forthcoming visit to the English capital. In an immediate reply, Burberrys regretted that the item had long since been disposed of, but that they would be delighted if Mr Joseph would join them for lunch and accept any jacket of his choice. This he duly did, and expressed himself satisfied that Burberry's assurance of their "best attention" had meant exactly that.

In the aftermath of his captivity, George Behling remembered: "I tried to forget. Obviously, I can't. Outside of the many bad nightmares and the devastating feeling of assault and infringement on my personal rights and freedom (akin, perhaps, to that felt by a rape victim) I came through mostly unscathed. And through the years it did make me impervious to many other so-called crises that I brushed off as trivia.

To the policeman who stopped me shortly after my return, for a minor traffic violation, looked in the car window and said, 'listen buddy, just because you're in that uniform doesn't mean that goes here,' you didn't notice me bite my lip or my hands grip the wheel while I fought back the urge to kill. After what I'd been through it wasn't worth winding up at a Court Martial or in a stockade over such a jerk as you.

To the many bartenders who refused me a drink, even a beer, because I wouldn't be 21 years old for another 5 months; you're forgiven—you only literally followed the law for your own protection."

In February 1994, a US National Public Radio report estimated that 70,000 ex-POWs were alive in America, more than 18,000 of whom had recurrent nightmares and other symptoms of post traumatic stress disorder. Others were tormented by what has become known as "survivor guilt".

BEHIND THE WIRE

ON NOVEMBER 2nd 1944, Roger Armstrong and the other crew members of the B-17G *Qualified Quail* were flying another aircraft, a nearly new, aluminum finish B-17. They were a part of the 91st Bomb Group and had taken up their assigned position near the end of the massive stream of 1,168 heavy bombers and their escort of 954 fighters. They were going out to hit a target in Merseberg, Germany, and their pilot, John Askins, was unfamiliar with this new plane, which seemed to Armstrong rather sluggish compared to the old *Quail*.

Roger had learned from the former navigator of this new plane that his crew voted on a name for it, but the name had not been painted on the nose before the crew had left on 48-hour pass to London. While they were gone the new bomber had become the mount of the Askins crew for this mission and during the night before the mission the name had been artfully applied: *U.S.A. The Hard Way*.

It would be a day Armstrong and the crew would never forget. The 91st put up thirty-seven bombers, of which thirty-six managed to attack the target. But thirteen failed to return from the raid: four shot down by enemy aircraft, two by anti-aircraft guns, one to accident, and the rest to unknown causes. Of the crews involved, forty-nine men were killed and 115 were missing in action. All thirteen B-17s downed were lost over enemy territory. It was the third highest loss the group had suffered in the entire war.

At their pre-mission briefing that day the airmen of the 91st were told that their target was defended by 372 flak guns and that they could expect a reception of at least seventy-five German fighters. As it happened, the enemy fighters, mostly FW-190s, raced into the bomber stream near the target as soon as the Allied fighter protection had been pulled off to go to the aide of other bomb groups.

The B-17 aircraft of the 91st had left the Bassingbourn base in formation at 9:50 that morning, climbing to reach a cruising altitude of 27,000 feet as they passed over the Zuider Zee. When it was formed the bomber stream was so long that it took more than thirty minutes to pass over a ground position. The enemy defences greatly surpassed the predicted response, with more than 400

German fighters arriving, determined to turn back the American raiders.

Radio-gunner Armstrong: "Just after crossing the German border, I switched to our fighter channel and heard the escort at the target warning, 'Bandits in the area!' I called John on the flight deck and asked if he or Randy were on the fighter channel. He replied: 'I am.' Then he called the crew and warned all of the gunners to be alert for fighters."

Robert Webb, ball-turret gunner: "I heard John's warning and immediately turned the ball 360 degrees, looking low and level, scanning the whole area under the ship. I saw two German Me 163s [rocket-propelled fighters] at 7:00 o'clock about two or three miles from the group. They then broke away and disappeared."

Armstrong: "Suddenly, I heard what sounded like 20mm cannon shells bursting in our ship. I looked up and out of the radio room ceiling window and saw we were about 700 to 800 feet below our assigned position. The plane then made what appeared to be a shallow bank to the left. No one had called out any fighters on the intercom. Something was definitely wrong. Usually the pilot would call and let us know if we were leaving the formation due to mechanical difficulties, but the intercom was silent.

"Then I noticed an odd odour in my oxygen mask. Looking at the oxygen regulator and gauge, I saw my pressure had dropped from a normal 400 lbs. to zero. I called the flight deck but got no answer. The intercom was not functioning. I opened the radio room door to the bomb bay and looked toward the flight deck. I saw fire.

"I noticed that John was in his seat with his right hand on the auto-pilot. Then another explosion and I could no longer see past the fire which by then was right at the front bulkhead of the bomb bay. I got out of my chair and unplugged my heated suit, removed my steel flak helmet, tore off my oxygen mask and left for the waist.

"As I passed the ball turret I saw that it was functioning, so I knew the electrical system must be OK. Then I saw Webb roll the turret up so his escape door was facing the top and it started to open. I looked toward the rear at Sergeant Harold Sackman and he was waving at me to come back. When I got to the waist door he shouted, 'It won't open!' We both struggled with it and found it had frozen shut due to the -40 degree temperature. Sackman then moved across the plane and dove into the door. It looked like a scene from the movies where a police officer breaks a door down with his shoulder. Both Sackman and the door flew out into space together.

"I looked back at the tail and Roy Loyless [tail gunner] was crawling toward his escape hatch. Then I looked toward the ball turret and could see the door open. I was getting anoxia from lack of oxygen and suddenly found I could not get my heavy flak suit off. So I sat down at the waist door, with my feet hanging out in the slipstream, took my right glove off and pulled the snaps loose at each shoulder. The suit fell off. Leaving my leather glove, I rolled out and immediately began tumbling over and over in space. I put my hands out and stabilized my body roll.

"I had practiced many times on missions, when there was not traffic on the radio, taking my mask, steel helmet and flak suit off, unhooking my heated suit and snapping my chute on the left ring of my harness. However, when you are not breathing enough oxygen the mind doesn't always function the way it should. We hadn't thought about an escape door frozen to the plane. So, I had expended too much energy, for the amount of oxygen I was breathing in that thin air at over 20,000 feet. Having left my right glove in the plane, I soon found that my right hand was getting very cold and when I reached the ground it was frost-bitten.

"We were high enough that we had sufficient time to work out anything we had forgotten to do. I realized that my chute was not hooked on the right ring, but I was falling free to get down quickly to where there was enough oxygen. After I fell approximately a mile, I decided it was about time to see if the chute would open. When I pulled the ripcord my feet were pointed toward the sky and my upper back and head toward the ground. The pilot chute popped out pulling the main chute from the pack on my chest. When the chute suddenly filled with air it cracked my body like a whip. Flight crews don't practice jumping from planes because if it doesn't work the first time, why practice? No one on our crew had been in a situation requiring a jump from an airplane. We had had a few lectures on the art of baling out, but that was about all.

"Once I cleared the plane there was no sensation of falling. It was deadly silent, except I could hear our plane about two miles to the east as it circled the crew. John had set the autopilot so the plane remained in a two to three degree bank, which allowed us to safely bale out. I looked down and saw four chutes below and looking up saw two above. We later learned that John delayed his jump, as instructed by Intelligence, to avoid being seen by the enemy. He pulled the ripcord when he saw the ground moving up, and swung once before his feet struck the top of a tree."

John Askins, pilot: "When we were hit, I didn't realize it was flak but thought it was an explosion from a leaking gas line near the top turret. The cockpit immediately filled with smoke and I couldn't see the instrument panel, lead ship, or the number two ship flying on our right side. There was no response on the yoke. I was able to reach the auto-pilot and steered the plane to the left, out of the formation, to avoid striking another plane." The pilot and copilot attempted to fight the fire on the flight deck but the hydraulic and oxygen lines had been severed. The engineer [Hilmer Beicker], who was in the top turret at the time, saw where the 88mm shell had exited the roof of the plane just behind the copilot's seat. It didn't explode over the plane. Fire was in the cockpit and turret as Beicker came out onto the flight deck. His clothing caught fire as one of the hydraulic lines with oxygen blowing on it was like a blowtorch. Beicker saw an explosion of flame. John put out the fire on Beicker's clothing but his parachute, which was lying near the turret, caught fire and popped open. One ring was burned off his parachute harness.

Beicker: "John stayed with me even though the oxygen bottles continued to blow up on the flight deck. He put the fire out on my chute and snapped both sides of it to the one ring on my harness. Then he helped me down to the nose where Randall Archer, our copilot who, along with Anthony Dela Porta, our navigator, pushed me out through the escape hatch. I hadn't heard the bail out bell. The wires had been severed."

When the pilot crawled down to the nose, everyone was gone so he jumped. Later, Armstrong saw Askins on the ground and noticed his eyebrows and hair were singed and his hands were burned.

Ball turret gunner Robert Webb: "I could hear the explosions on the flight deck, down in the ball. As I turned the turret to 12:00

o'clock and I counted three bodies come out of the nose hatch. Then smoke was coming from the nose hatch and I decided it was time to leave." Webb had his chute with him in the ball. When he left the turret, he went up to look in the bomb bay. By then fire had reached the bombs. He hurried back to the waist and baled out, the last crew member to leave the stricken plane.

Webb: "I saw three bursts of flak, from a tower in the woods below. I didn't see the fourth burst, but it hit and entered the ship slightly ahead of the top turret."

Webb landed in the forest and immediately realized he had brought his wallet with him on the mission. They had just been paid. He quickly buried the wallet under a tree. Fishing in his other pockets he found some fake bread ration stamps which he also buried, not wanting to be found with them if he were captured.

When Roy Loyless jumped from the waist hatch the jolt of his chute opening and the lack of oxygen caused him to lose consciousness. When he awoke a few minutes later, four P-51 Mustang escort fighters were circling him. They began coming in too close and as they passed were spilling the air from his chute. He motioned for them to leave as they kept collapsing his chute. They understood and moved out some distance. The Mustangs did not have their wing tanks. They were on there way back to their 9th Air Force base in France.

Loyless landed in the trees, hung up on a limb fifteen feet above the ground. A group of children soon gathered around the tree along with four German air force women. Loyless heard the children speaking English in conversation with the women. At last he was able to cut himself free from his parachute harness and drop to the ground. One of the boys said "You are an American, yes?" Loyless nodded. Another of the boys said "These girls are flak gunners. They shot your plane down. Roy asked the boys "Would you climb the tree and get my chute for me?" One of them did so, freeing the chute and letting it drop to the ground.

Within minutes some German farmers arrived carrying pitchforks and shotguns. They took him to a nearby bed-and-breakfast home. Three German officers were sitting at a table and they took Loyless to the crash sight of his B-17. Loyless: "The plane had exploded on impact, due to the fuel remaining in the tanks. Maps were scattered around; the life rafts had inflated and were up in the treetops, but the bombs had not gone off. The nose section was lying on its side. On it was painted a girl trying to hitch a ride to America, and the name U.S.A. The Hard Way." Loyless told the German officers "We shouldn't stay around here. One of the delayed-action bombs may go off at any minute." His warning caused the Germans to quickly lose interest in examining the maps and charts by the aircraft.

Loyless: "I looked in the tail section and saw that my shoes, the ones I took on all missions, were still sitting in the exact spot where I had placed them. I always tied them together because one shoe is just as bad as having none. When I got back to the German truck, I put on my G.I. shoes and gave my flying boots to one of the German officers.

Armstrong: "When our plane crashed I was descending through approximately 6,500 feet. The explosion caused my chute to suddenly rise, giving me a weird feeling in my stomach. I heard machine-gun fire, but when I looked around I could see no other planes. I guessed it was our .50-caliber ammo cooking off from the heat of the fire. White and black smoke rose from the scene of the crash and I hoped no bodies were in it, as I had counted only seven of the nine chutes that should have been in the air."

Roy Loyless assumed that the three German officers would take him to a nearby base, but they took him back to the bed-and-breakfast and left him there. His parachute was lying in a corner of the room and he picked it up and gave it to the lady who owned the house. She was happy to have all that nylon material. Then one of the shotgun-toting farmers ordered Roy into the back of a horse-drawn wagon and drove him to a nearby town. Loyless thought about overpowering the man, but believing the war would probably be over within a matter of days, decided against it.

Armstrong: "As I floated down I had seen nothing but a huge forest below. Then I saw a large lake and the wind was carrying me out over the water. I reached for my Boy Scout knife and began thinking about the possibility of drowning as my wet chute pulled me under. My Mae West life vest was under my parachute harness. I thought about unsnapping my harness around my thighs, but could not get the snaps loose. My leg straps were too tight. It was fortunate that I was unsuccessful as I would have fallen out of my harness. Then the wind shifted and I was blown away from the lake.

"As I dropped closer to the ground, it finally dawned on me that I was not landing among friends! But I was very thankful that there were no large cities nearby that had been bombed by the RAF or the U.S. Air Corps. As I dropped below 1,000 feet I smelled kraut cooking. I looked at my watch. It was 12 noon. And then I saw the ground coming up rapidly; it was my first sensation of falling. Fortunately, I landed on a grass trail in the woods. My chute must have lightly touched a tree, dumping the air out of it.

"When my chute had opened, I noticed that there were no risers, the web straps that are normally attached to each ring of the harness. Mine was a British-made chute. On American chutes the shroud lines were attached to the top of each riser. You could then reach up and control your chute direction of travel by pulling on the risers. If you pulled on the right riser you would slip to the right as a result of dumping air out of the left side of the chute. If you pulled on the left riser you slid to the left. You could also turn yourself around by crossing your arms and pulling on the left riser with your right hand and the right riser with your left hand. Thus, you had some control over the chute. You always wanted to keep the wind at your back so that you would not land striking the back of your head. And you could slip your chute to the right or the left to avoid an obstacle such as a tree, a telephone pole or a church steeple.

"Our parachute chest packs were made by the Irvin Air Chute Company of Letchworth, England, and when our lives were saved by their parachutes, we became eligible for membership in the exclusive 'Caterpillar Club. The Irvin company then enrolled you and sent you a card and a gold caterpillar pin with your name engraved on the back.

"I struck the ground with the wind in my face, resulting in my legs giving way. This caused me to fall back, striking my buttocks and then the back of my head. The impact stunned me and for a few minutes I lay there until my head cleared. When I got up I realized I had pulled a groin muscle which had happened when my chute opened. Not having risers on the chute, I had to live with my problem until I hit the ground.

"Now that I realized where I was, I started thinking about evasion. I got up, headed into the woods, and stopped. I had left my chute lying on the trail. As I hurried back, my knee buckled, causing me to pull up and stop. I limped back to where my chute lay, and my thoughts of a successful evasion began to slip away. Would I be able to walk any great distance? Some of the men appeared to be members of the Home Guard. They took Askins to the village of Bippen.

Armstrong: "As I stooped over to gather up my parachute, I heard someone in the woods holler 'Halt!' There was a man in his late sixties with a rifle leveled at me. I held my hands up and looked at the large German Shepherd dog standing beside him. He said something to the dog and it came charging at me, barking and snarling. When the dog was about fifteen feet from me, the man shouted something in German and the dog stopped. He then turned his head toward his master, then back at me and began to snarl again. He worried me more than the man with the gun.

"The man was a member of the Volksturm, the People's Home Guard formed near the end of the war and consisting of men and boys who were unable to serve in the regular army. He was wearing an old German Army coat and hat but had on a pair of civilian pants and his own high-top leather boots. The rifle appeared to be of World War One vintage. While the dog stood drooling and growling, my captor approached with caution. The dog was angry because his master had not released him from his order to stop. My captor asked me, in German, who I was; then said 'English?'

"I replied, 'No. I am an American.' He then pointed to himself and said 'Deutsch.' I remembered that Tony said we had just crossed the German border from the Netherlands. I thought the man said he was Dutch. I already had my escape kit in my hand and pointed to a phrase on the card that said 'CAN YOU HIDE ME? ' This didn't strike him as humorous. He knocked the translation card from my hand and asked 'Veapon?' I finally realized that he wanted to know if I was carrying a gun. He indicated that I should empty my pockets. When he saw my Boy Scout knife he got excited and shouted 'Veapon!' Then he pocketed my knife and pointed down the grassy trail, indicating he wanted me to walk in that direction. He made sure that I brought my parachute with me and I folded it up so I wouldn't trip over the shroud lines.

"As we walked on the grass trail through the trees, I wondered what kind of reception awaited me when we got to the road. When we got there it was paved with asphault and marked for two lanes. There were shallow grassy ditches on each side. My guard then indicated I should walk in a northerly direction. I then saw, about a quarter of a mile north of us, a group of people headed south. Leading the procession of thirty to forty villagers was a man on a bicycle. He was followed by three or four members of the German infantry.

"The portly older man on the bike was the obvious leader as he was wearing his steel helmet from World War One. It had a spike on top. He was dressed in his WWI uniform which had a frock tail coat. It buttoned up the back so he could ride a horse or bicycle. He was also wearing a red arm band with a swastika inside a white circle. He was not only a WWI veteran but also a party member. He was wearing riding breeches and boots. On one side of his highly polished belt was a holster with a Walther automatic pistol. The other side of his belt held a ceremonial sword in a silver scabbord, clearly WWI issue. The sword kept getting into the spokes of the bike which caused a lot of grins and silent laughs behind his back. The infantry men were making light of the effect he was obviously trying to have on the villagers and me.

"The infantry men were wearing their regulation green uniforms. They all seemed to be in their late teens or early twenties. I soon learned that the leader was not only head of the local Nazi party, but the Chief of Police as well.

"As the local chief approached my captor and me, he looked down to extract his sword from his front wheel, and his shiny helmet fell off and bounced toward us on the road. He brought his bike to a halt and huffed and puffed trying to raise his leg over the frame. He started to fall, but was saved by the infantry men and his little army of four doubled over, holding their hands over the mouths to keep from laughing. The villagers were smiling. With his helmet on the pavement, I saw he had a crew cut of salt and pepper grey and brown hair. He also sported a Hitler mustache. As his helmet was handed back to him, one of the troops could no longer contain himself and laughed out loud, which got him a severe tongue-lashing from his chief whose red face made him look like he was having a stroke. It was my first encounter with a German in authority yelling at the top of his lungs at one of his subordinates.

"The chief shouted an order to the infantry men and his villagers and they headed back to the village. He and his infantry escort walked behind my captor and me. He didn't try to ride his bike on the return trip, having 'lost face' trying to ride it to the scene of the prisoner capture. He could no longer hide his anger so he tried to alleviate his frustrations by shoving his bike into my behind. As we walked toward the village of Bippen, a little girl came over and walked beside me for a few minutes. She finally got up her courage and said 'Are you from Chicago?' I said 'No.' She then asked 'Are you a gangster?' I said 'No. I am an American.' 'Do you know what Hitler says about American flyers?' 'No, I don't' I replied. 'He says all American flyers are gangsters and are from Chicago.' 'Hitler is not telling the truth' said I. 'Don't you receive $1,000 American dollars to fly over our country and bomb our houses?' said she. 'No' said I. 'Where did you learn to speak such good English?' 'All German children study the English language in school' said she. I then said 'I would like to visit with you, but by the rules of war, signed by Germany and America, I can't talk with you.' She looked disappointed but I smiled at her and she rejoined her mother.

"I then heard the engine sound of two P-47 Thunderbolt fighters and knew they were down on the deck. One flew over the woods parallel to the road, northbound at about 250 mph. I looked around and saw that I was the only person standing in the road. Then I saw his wingman, covering him at about 400 feet above us. The flight leader pulled up slightly, made a 180 degree turn and came back, flying down the other side of the road. As he approached I could hear his engine running at a much slower speed. He was just maintaining airspeed. He dropped out of sight south of us, due to the tall trees, but I noted his wingman was making a large circle, sweeping the area, looking for hostile planes and anti-aircraft positions.

"Suddenly the leader came northbound on the right side of the road, motioning as if asking whether I wanted him to strafe the woods. I looked and saw five rifles and the chief's Walther aimed at me. The Thunderbolt leader came back in a long, slow bank, pointing one of his fingers down. I dropped my chute and placed both my hands on my head. The pilot came around again and shook his head up and down indicating he understood. He circled once again and held up his left hand making a V for victory sign. Then on his next pass buzzed at high speed, pulled up in a steep climb; his wingman joined up and they headed west. He undoubtedly had seen the smoke from our downed plane and saw me in the road with the Germans around. I was lucky my white chute was in my arms as he easily identified me as an American flyer.

"My German escort now came out of the woods. The little girl who had talked to me said 'Jabo [fighter bomber] bombed our school last week.' I knew she meant P-47s, which our people referred to as 'Jugs' because they resembled a flying milk bottle. I was probably the first American they had seen since their school was allegedly bombed. I imagined I would see a tree in the village square with a rope and a hangman's noose at the end.

"As we walked toward the village I noticed there was some animosity between the chief and the infantry. I hoped the infantry would assume control over me when we reached a town. As we entered the village, I saw a road sign with the name Bippen on it. I saw the schoolhouse that had been completely destroyed. It looked to me as if it had been used to store ammunition. S-2 had told us that some German schools and hospitals were being used for that purpose.

"The village looked like a picture postcard scene out of Grimm's Fairy Tales. They marched me up the main street to the home of the Chief of Police, a small red brick house trimmed in fresh white paint. There was a pretty white picket fence around the front lawn and some late-blooming flowers in flower boxes. In front of the house was a pole on which a Nazi flag was flying.

"I was taken into the hall and noticed that there were two parachutes lying on the floor in front of a closed door to the front room. A woman wearing an apron opened the kitchen door and I smelled cabbage cooking. The floors were solid oak and had recently been waxed. The house was immaculate. Having seen the two parachutes, I was wondering who might be there from our crew. I entered the front room with one of the infantry men. Sitting on one side was our pilot, John Askins, and on the other side waist gunner Harold Sackman. None of us spoke to each other as we didn't want them to know we were from the same crew. About thirty minutes later, our bombardier, Paul Collier, was brought in by another German infantry man.

"The chief had his desk in the front room. It faced the front windows, so his back was to us. Two of the infantry men stayed in the room, armed with rifles. They finally sat down and watched us while the chief ceremoniously phoned a Luftwaffe base. When he lifted the French-style phone to make the call, he did so in a military manner. He lifted the phone straight up out of the cradle, stopped, then moved his arm in a straight line to ear and mouth. It would have been humourous but for the uncertainty of our future. The infantry guards were amused watching the eccentric manner in which the chief was reporting his important findings to the Luftwaffe. He made copious notes in his record book as he completed each task.

"Now there were four of us in the chief's home. The German Air Force had been notified about us and we were finally turned over to the infantry guards who took us down the main street to what appeared to be an empty store. One of the men was left to guard the four of us. He was a young, red-headed friendly type who sat at the front of the store. His English was quite good. He wanted to know when the war was going to be over. We said 'In another two or three weeks at the most.' He asked 'How badly has New York been bombed?' One of us said 'It hasn't' He said 'We have a new six-engine bomber that has been bombing the U.S.A.' We hadn't heard about it and never considered they had the capability to fly a plane that far and back. It had actually been considered, but put on the back burner by Hitler. It was to be known as the Me-264. Göring referred to it as the 'New York bomber.' But the building of the Me-262 jet fighter took priority over other planes on the drawing boards.

"Our guard wanted to know about the food in England and we told him we had all the steak and eggs we could eat. There was an old picture of Hitler on the wall near where our guard sat. He got up, went over to the picture and turned it around so Hitler faced the wall. Later in the afternoon, the young guard said 'Hitler has a secret weapon which will win the war for Germany.' We told him he was misinformed, but not quite in that language.

"Around five p.m., some slave labourers came in from the fields. They had heard of our capture and one of them, a tall Frenchman, asked our guard if he could bring us some food. The young German said it would be OK. The Frenchman came back with an apple for each of us.

Evening approached and the four prisoners lay down on their parachutes and tried to get some sleep. Around midnight three Luftwaffe guards from a nearby base walked in the front door. Armstrong: " They carried machine-pistols and, to impress us, held their guns up to the light and charged them, throwing a bullet into the chamber. Then they motioned for us to get up, but to leave our parachutes where they were. One of them, a young, black-eyed sergeant who was very impressed with himself and very arrogant ordered us firmly. We moved out into the night, not knowing where we were being taken. The moon was bright and our eyes soon became accustomed to the darkness.

"As we walked toward the village train station, we were aware of the ground sparkling. I was fascinated by how the RAF and the 8th Air Force had decorated the country with chaff [aluminium foil strips dropped to confuse enemy radar]. We now knew that we were in an area where our bombers could have been on a run for one of the nearby industrial cities. We were very careful not to comment on it in front of our guards. Osnabruck, one of the Allied targets, was about twenty to thirty miles southeast of Bippen and it was logical that the bomb groups started their bomb runs in the area of this village. Munster was another prime target about fifty miles south of Osnabruck.

"The train station was blacked out and there were no lights showing in the area. As the train pulled into the station, we saw that it was not lighted. The guards directed us to a third class car. I saw that the engine was pulling only three or four passenger cars. We were obviously not on one of the main lines of the German Railway System.

"There were long wooden benches on each side of the car so the passengers faced each other. The three guards sat facing us. We were the only passengers. The toughest-looking guard sat directly across from me. He held his machine-pistol in his lap and aimed right at my stomach. This made me nervous, so I slowly slid to my left but the gun barrel followed my progress. The bright moonlight was enough to illuminate the car.

"The train proceeded slowly for about an hour until we reached a good-sized town. John and I guessed that it was Oldenburg. When the train stopped, the guards motioned for us to get off. We then walked to what resembled a county jail in a small American town. Our jailers were expecting us and we assumed the Luftwaffe had cut orders for our trip to the interrogation center. We were turned over to what looked like a mixed Command, as there were infantry and SS officers present. In the front of the prison was a fair-sized room with bunks lining the four walls. This turned out to be the night lock-up for the local slave labourers from various nations overrun by the German Army.

"The jail was built of red bricks. In the back we found we were placed in cells with heavy solid wood doors. Each door had a small hole in it which was used by the guards to periodically check on what you were doing during the night and day. We were to be in solitary confinement.

"In the entry hall was a desk with an SS captain behind it. He looked me up and down and said 'Halt!' The other three crew members were taken away by a guard, but I could not see which cells they were put in. In guteral English, the SS captain said 'Take off your boots!' I had no alternative but to give up my flying boots. I knew he wanted them for himself. This left me with only the felt inserts containing the wires that were attached to my heated suit. I did have a pair of socks under the felt inserts, but hoped I wouldn't have to do too much walking.

"A guard took me to a vacant cell. The walls were of solid wood and I figured they were probably reinforced by steel bars. The cell was about ten feet long and five feet wide. If you stood on the bed you could see out of the one window on the outside wall. The bed was of wood, with no mattress, springs or padding. The pillow was made of wood and was about three inches higher than the bed. The pillow was made of two 2x4s with a small plank of wood connecting them. There was no padding. It was truly 'a headboard.'

"As soon as the cell door was slammed shut by the guard, he turned the light bulb off. I had seen one thin, grey blanket at the bottom of the bed before he shut the door. I couldn't decide whether to sleep on it or put it over me. As I lay on the bed, I finally became aware that I was actually in prison. And to make it worse, in solitary confinement.

"Yesterday we were engaged in a very impersonal war. Now, I have no idea where the other five members of our crew are, or if they are still alive. The only thing I am sure about is that I am in jail in northwest Germany, but I am not sure of the name of the town.

"Lying there in the dark, I thought about the prisoner-of-war lectures we had been given, which I later learned were quite accurate. But I was not certain that I would ever make it to a POW camp, much less one known to exist by the International Red Cross. With no Luftwaffe personnel in the office of the jail, I wasn't sure we were under their jurisdiction. I only knew that some Luftwaffe base knew of us as they had escorted us to this jail.

"I had just drifted off to sleep when the light in the cell was turned on and I could see movement at the hole in the door. It was the worst moment of my life; the first time I had been with people who were actually my enemy. It had now become a very personal war for me. I wondered then if we had killed any of these people's wives, children, mothers or fathers. At that moment, I had absolutely no control over my own life. I thought of those POW lectures when we were told, at this late stage in the war, to 'avoid large cities and keep away from the civilian population. Get to the military as soon as you can, if you are in Germany and can't speak the language. There is no underground in Germany to help you. There are death zones where anyone found without papers will be shot.'

"Early the next morning the sun was shining through the small window in my cell. I stood on my wooden pillow and looked out. The view reminded me of a movie in which the enemy was caught and imprisoned. The yard was surrounded by brick walls with large pieces of glass embedded on top. I could see the Germans marching us out, asking if we wanted a blindfold as we faced the firing squad. I put that thought out of my mind as I heard a faint tapping on the wall across from my bed. I realized it was Morse code so I tapped back asking who was in the cell.

"The reply was 'John.' 'It's Roger. Any information?' The reply was negative, but it lifted my spirits to know that John and I could converse. It was November 3rd 1944.

"The door opened and a German infantry guard escorted a young man into the cell. He was a blond teenager wearing a black turtleneck sweater. He came to my bed and handed me a piece of black German bread with some kind of red jam on it. He also gave me a cup of water. He seemed to be deaf, as the guard motioned for him to leave the cell when I had been served. The young man had a blank stare on his face and appeared to be mentally retarded. I tasted the bread and found it sour and bitter. It was very heavy for bread. I couldn't force myself to eat, so I hid it under the blanket, thinking that if they discovered I was not eating my bread, they might not bring any more food. It never occurred to me that I would acquire a taste for the sour, evil-smelling stuff.

"About fifteen minutes later, the door opened again and a guard motioned for me to walk ahead of him. We passed about twenty cells but I couldn't tell if they were occupied. The guard took me to a foul bathroom where I was not allowed to shave, but could take care of other physical needs.

"At noon the same young man arrived, this time with a bowl of hot chicken soup. On closer examination, I found it contained the digestive tract of the fowl. When my jailers returned, the bowl was still full. I tried sipping the soup, but the contents had spread their flavour throughout. The guard frowned and I lifted part of the contents out. He didn't like what he saw and motioned for the boy to remove the bowl. Neither of them returned.

"In the late afternoon the door opened again and the guard motioned for me to leave the cell. I was taken to what seemed to be the office of the jail. It was a very happy occasion, as there were seven of my crew members. But Randall Archer, our copilot, was not among them. To that point, I was only certain that John, Paul, Harold and I had survived the jump from the plane. We were very glad to see Roy, Robert, Tony and Hilmer. At first glance we saw that Hilmer obviously had a broken leg. We didn't realize how badly he was injured until later. We all wondered about Archer. Had he been killed in the fall; tried to escape; was he hiding out? Beicker told of hearing the shooting down the road and we believed Archer might be dead.

"Then we noticed four Luftwaffe guards standing near us. One had a set of orders which he showed to both an infantry officer and an SS officer. After some papers were signed, the sergeant in charge of our escort motioned for us to follow him, with the other three guards bringing up the rear. Our Luftwaffe guards had orders to escort us to the Interrogation Center known as Auswertestelle West. It was located at Oberursel, about ten miles north of Frankfurt-on-

Main.

"All of our German guards appeared to be very powerful men. The sergeant in charge was the largest and seemed to be the toughest. They wore blue uniforms. Each carried a knapsack on his back; two carried burp guns and two carried rifles. They all carried side arms. These guns were not only to prevent our escape; but to protect us from the civilian population. We soon learned that the knapsacks contained food for our guards and us.

"It became apparent that Beicker had more than a fractured leg, which was in itself bad enough. He also had fractured ribs, clavicle and jaw. The cast on his leg was bothering him because it wasn't enough support for the break, and he later learned that the leg hadn't been properly set. The German doctor, who had put the cast on Beicker, didn't give him crutches. It was obvious that he couldn't have used them, with a fractured clavicle and his painful ribs. So, we used our Boy Scout training and carried him between two of us. We crossed our arms and formed a chair. When we learned the German guards couldn't speak English, Beicker translated for us. This worked well until he became weary, with no pain killers to help. Later he told us his jaw was fractured, which made it difficult to speak. He was a very stoic person.

"When the train stopped at Oberursel station, we were turned over to guards from the interrogation center. We were also met by an interpreter for the walk to the center. He told us to form up four abreast in formation. I noticed other crews, partial crews, individual crew members and fighter pilots. Our interpreter's instructions were: 'Please do not talk, smile or look around. Look straight ahead or look down, and do not whistle at the girls as we pass by.

"A fine mist was coming down, which caused the streets to become wet and slippery. For the first time, I realized the importance of having a pair of shoes. All I had on my feet were the felt inserts to my heated suit. It was fall and the leaves were starting to turn and it was getting cold.

"When we reached the camp the sun had set but it was not yet completely dark. This was the last time I would see my crew members for many months.

"On entering the Luftwaffe Evaluation Center, I regretted I had not learned more about the rules governing prisoners of war. S-2 had the best evidence of what would happen to a downed airman. I found they had conveyed as much as they knew. I am certain that the treatment we received was based on the fact that many German POWs were held in the U.S.A., Canada, and England. The Geneva Convention was the birthplace of the modern rules on the handling of prisoners of war. I had not realized that a number of countries had signed it as long ago as 1864. I did not know that it was in effect during WWI and that Germany, England, and the United States were signatories. The question of every potential POW was, will they live up to the 'spirit of the Convention rules?'

"I was photographed as if a mug shot was being taken by the police. The photo was later placed on my personal POW record card. The photographer used a tripod with a Leica 35mm camera. As I looked into the camera I silently cursed the man taking my photograph. I also hoped I could find such a camera at the end of the war. Before taking my picture he wrote my serial number in chalk on a blackboard that he hung around my neck.

"A guard then took me to solitary confinement which consisted of a 5x9 cell containing a bed with about one inch of straw stuffed into what appeared to be a large gunny sack. I had been in my cell for about an hour when the door opened and two guards walked in accompanying my interrogator. The man wore a pleasant smile and said 'For you the war is over.'

IN THE BAG

IN HIS BOOK, *Stalag Luft III*, about the lives and experiences of the Allied prisoners of war in what may be the most famous and notorious European POW camp of the Second World War, the eminent historian and author Arthur A. Durand wrote of the "main priority" for many of the more than 10,000 men who had found themselves residents there by the end of that war. Their priority was the planning and execution of escapes that would aid the Allied war effort by undermining German military resources. The prime example of those efforts was what has come to be known as "the Great Escape", a mass operation in which seventy-six prsioners made a dramatic bid for freedom during the night of 24-25 March 1944.

As the note on the back cover of his book states: "Based largely on a coded diary kept secretly by the prisoners, *Stalag Luft III* provides the complete picture of life inside the camp. Historian Arthur A. Durand also draws on other firsthand sources—both Allied and German—including interviews, diaries, letters, and recently declassified government documents. Durand has provided a masterly re-creation of virtually every aspect of the daily prison experience and a testament to the prisoners' ingenuity, perseverance, and raw courage against monumental odds."

From *Stalag Luft III*, reprinted by permission of Arthur A. Durand: "When Colonel Delmar T. Spivey entered Stalag Luft III in late July, 1943, he was a full colonel and twice the age of most of his fellow inmates. The senior staff immediately realized that his seniority and West Point training would catapult him into prominece as a leader. To reduce the chances of his inadvertently giving away important secrets to the Germans, the staff quickly briefed him on the entire spectrum of camp activities, including the vital covert intelligence and escape work that had been painfully developed during the three years since the first Allied fliers were captured by the Germans.

"Spivey stood transfixed as he looked into the gaping hole of the entrance shaft to tunnel 'Harry.' It descended thirty feet straight down, shored every inch of the way with bed boards taken by quota from the prisoners. He was told also about its overall design—

projected three-hundred-foot length,electric lights, self-contained storage and work rooms, and specially designed railroad trolleys to carry the dirt back out of the tunnel as it was being dug. He was even more surprised to learn that the tunnel he was staring at was but one of three such undertakings, and that the entire effort was tightly orchestrated by an interesting character code-named Big X. During succeeding days he learned all about the prisoners' forgery operation, covert communications with London and Washington, impressive education and theatrical programs, and robust play on the athletic fields.

"Two weeks later Spivey assumed command as Senior American Officer (SAO) of Center Compound. Still dazzled by what he had seen, he reflected on the need to record for posterity the amazing activities he saw at every turn. If nothing else, he reasoned, the account might make it easier for the next generation of prisoners and save them the trouble of having to 'invent the wheel all over again.' As logical and intriguing as the idea sounded, Spivey knew there were great risks. The Germans obviously would love to get their hands on so revealing a document. He nonetheless decided to proceed with the effort, knowing that everything hinged on the careful observance of numerous precautions and safeguards.

"As a first step he appointed three lieutenants to serve as compound historians: Thomas E. Mulligan, Lyman B. Burbank, and Robert R. Brunn. Their task was to record and enter into a log everything of significance that happened each day. To preclude the log's falling into German hands in any useable form, certain information was coded by means of a simple but effective technique. After the three men agreed on the items to be recorded and were satisfied with the way it all looked on paper, they initiated a clever routine. One man took the first word of the text and every third word thereafter and wrote them on a sheet of paper without any capitalization or punctuation. The second man started with the second word and did likewise, and the third man wrote down every third word. The three strings of nonsensical prose, of an by themselves, meant nothing and revealed nothing. The three sheet of paper were then hidden in separate locations, some in hollowed-out table legs, others in prepared wall cavities, and still others found their way into nooks and crannies of every imaginable description. There they remained until the camp was hastily evacuated in late January

1945. They were gathered up and transported westward with great effort and considerable risk as the Germans marched the prisoners away from the rapidly advancing Russian armies.

"Albert P. Clark, Jr., answered to the nickname Bub. But he also answered to either Junior, which many thought more appropriate in view of his youthful appearance, or Red for his flaming hair. Tall and thin, Bub responded good-naturedly even when someone called him Flamingo—at times his lanky legs did seem to bend a little backwards at the knees. The nicknames in part described and in part belied the character of the man. Behind his kid's grin and youthful looks was an officer who rightfully wore the insignia of a lieutenant colonel at the early age of twenty-seven. Outwardly shy and unassuming, Bub was a quiet, self-assured leader who could be effective without drawing attention to himself—the kind of man one would like to see in the intelligence business. In the early summer of 1942, however, that sort of work was probably the farthest thing from Bub's mind. His full attention at the time was devoted to surviving as a fighter pilot under the tutelage of the veterans of the Battle of Britain.

"Fighter pilots must be prepared to fight alone. Bub knew that and had the constitution for it. But common sense and experience told fighter pilots and bomber crews alike that the enemy would be quick to gang up on any plane found beyond the protective firepower of its parent formation. In spite of their best efforts, however, fliers did sometimes find themselves alone and, not unexpectedly, outnumbered. It happened to many. Lieutenant Colonel Clark was one of them.

"On Sunday, July 26, 1942, members of the 31st Fighter Group, to which Clark was assigned, were ordered to conduct a sweep over the Continent, the objective being to surprise and destroy the enemy in his own territory. The target area, Abbeville, France, was one of the primary bases of the Richthofen Geschwader and its one thousand German fighters then deployed along the coast.

"Just off the French coast, the Spitfires climbed rapidly to eighteen thousand feet. Wing Commander Johnny Walker broke radio silence, asking for the location of enemy fighters. RAF radar reported '50 plus' Focke-Wulfs above the invading force. The element of surprise clearly lost, the entire formation entered a 180-degree left turn over Abbeville. Suddenly the Canadian commander of Yellow Flight, with Clark as Yellow Two, spotted an attractive target— German aircraft taxiing on the runway. He peeled off, and Bub followed quickly. The switch in direction occurred so abruptly that Yellow Three and Four never really caught up. One German aircraft apparently went down, but Yellow One obviously did not stay around to confirm the kill. Knowing he had flown into a hornet's nest, he slammed the throttle to emergency power. Again Clark had to play catch-up, but by now the gap between them had become too great. He was on his own.

"Instinctively Clark headed straight for the sea at full throttle, fifty feet off the ground In spite of the advantage he seemed to have over the enemy fighters, several FW-190s soon closed in and scored one hit in his left wing, cutting the ram-air supply to his airspeed indicator. The needle stuck on 320 mph. Bub called for assistance, but no one responded. Yellow One, Three and Four were nowhere in sight. In desperation, Clark made a tight 180-degree turn, engaged in two head-on firing exchanges, then made another run for the sea. Crossing the coast, he was jolted by flak and found four more aircraft gaining on him. Bullets fired by his pursuers created tiny water spouts all around the low-flying Spitfire. With Clark almost clipping the waves, the enemy could not gain an altitude advantage and still go after him. Knowing the FW-190 was faster than the Spitfire at sea level, Clark did a sudden loop and came down on the tails of a pair of FWs breaking right. He emptied his guns at them. The other pair, apparently shaken by his surprise move, broke left, and all four flew off. Somewhat relieved after all the jinking, Clark also headed for home—land was in sight, presumably the English side of the Channel. He saw no more German aircraft, but suddenly had another crisis. The engin began to fail with high engine performance readings, apparently from being operated for so long at full emergency power.

"The running battle had carried Bub some distance out to sea. And the Spitfire was a notoriously rapid sinker. He recalled all too vividly that exactly one week earlier the distinguished Irish ace, Paddy Finucane, had been seen alive and well in the cockpit as his Spitfire settled on the water. But it sank in the fleeting moment before the pilot could escape. Bub quickly gave a Mayday call and attempted to jettison the cockpit canopy. The rusted jettison handle broke in his hand. The canopy would not open. Turning directly toward land, he put his feet on the dash in preparation for whatever came next. Dead ahead lay the low bluffs that shield the coast just south of Cap Gris-Nez near Ambleteuse, Pas de Calais, France. The Spitfire maintained barely enough airspeed to clear the bluff before crashing into a field. Shaken and exhausted, Clark struggled once again with the canopy, got it open, and leapt out. Greeted immediately by German soldiers manning the coastal gun batteries, he sadly realized that there was no place to go. Having faced the enemy alone in the air, he now faced them alone on the ground. Like so many of his colleagues, he had found the gateway to prison.

"War is full of surprises, but few are welcome. Clark could vouch for that—and his experience certainly was not unusual. Until their own planes were hit, most airmen engaging the enemy felt they were mere observers at a bizarre satanic affair. All around rained death and destruction, which for some inexplicable reason were passing them by. As if in a dream they watched other unfortunate airmen plunge to fiery deaths, amid debris and ruin, mangled and bloody. With tightened stomachs and sweating hands they watched in awe . . . and waited . . . methodically and frantically engaged in the mechanics of combat but nonetheless suspended in time. At times they almost wished the seemingly inevitable would come, so the uncertainty would end and their long awaited fate would at last be revealed. They prepared as best they could for the madness, steeling themselves physically and emotionally, knowing all along that their preparations were anything but adequate. Surprises occurred, usually in rapid succession, and were almost always bad ones—a fact of life for airmen. Only on the rarest occaisions did fliers find otherwise. First Lieutenant Norman L. Widen, known as Cy, was one of the few who did.

"There were two things almost everyone knew about Cy: he was always hungry, and he was afraid of water. Flying a single seat P-38 as an escort for John Morely Bennett's B-17 bomber flight when the formation crossed the North Atlantic, and later during orientation operations around the coast of England, Cy busied his mind with ways to survive in the event he was hit. He could not swim, and water bothered him. Like the Spitfire, he was a natural-born sinker.

"Cy had little confidence in the sea survival gear provided at that time by the United States Army Air Forces, which consisted primarily of a navy-type inflatable dinghy and the standard inflatable Mae West life jacket. He was impressed, however, with the equipment provided to British crewmen. So when the American gear left him floundering during routine training in a swimming pool, he knew what he had to do. A quick midnight requisition gave him a British Mae West that contained special flotation devices in addition to a better mechanism for oral inflation if the CO2 cartridge did not work. He also obtained a British dinghy and outfitted it with survival aids he thought would be helpful: a flourescien dye to repel sharks and visually assist rescue planes, a whistle for summoning surface vessels, a mirror to shine toward aircraft that might be searching for him, a skull cap with a yellow visible from above, a can of bully beef and some iron pills for strength, a little telescoping flag to signal surface vessels, a flashlight with an extra bulb, a .45 automatic pistol, a razor, a toothbrush, and photographs that could be pasted on false identity cards. Then in the extra dinghy he sat on he carried a machete, a first-aid kit, a compass, maps, fishhooks, and a water bag. He even made sure he had a British parachute. In the water it took two hands to unfasten the American chute; the British had redesigned theirs so that one hand could release it in two quick movements. Perhaps some of his fellow fliers thought him a little too cautious. Actually he was only being prudent. Thousands of crewmen lived to curse the day they failed to make such preparations.

"On December 18, 1942, Cy climbed into his P-38 in North Africa to fly cover for a bombing mission against a nearby docking facility on the Tunisian coast. Cy's place was clearly marked, the ground crew having painted Great Gut in large letters on one boom and Chow Hound on the other in affectionate recognition of his constant longing for food. Noting a malfunction as he ran up the engines, Cy opted for another plane. Unfortunately, it was not much better. Apprehensive from the start, he nonetheless took his place in the formation.

"At about 31,000 feet the fighters were jumped by Me-109s. In the dogfight that ensued, Cy maneuvred into position and hammered bullets into an enemy fighter with telling effect. The Me-109 strggled for a time, but then went down. Cy did not see the outcome. While still zeroed in on his quarry, he felt the sudden impact of enemy fire striking his own left engine and looked up just in time to see it burst into flames. At the same time he saw the pursuing Me-109 and immediately started sharp inside turns to shake it off. But the thickening smoke and flames creeping into the cockpit warned him he had to get out—and soon.

"Getting out of a burning, twisting P-38 was a fighter pilot's nightmare. The booms were connected in the rear by a horizontal stabilizer mounted directly in the path of an ejecting body caught in the windstream of the plummeting aircraft. Since there was no powered ejection seat, the best a pilot could do was turn the aircraft upside down and slide out with just enough downward motion to slip under the stabilizer or with enough force to go over it. Unfortunately, Cy's plane was already in a screaming dive and out of control. He could no longer turn it over, but hoped he could slide under the cleaver that would be slicing toward him the instant he left the cockpit. Seconds counted now. As he released the canopy and stood up, a 400-mph wind slammed and tore at him as he struggled to kick free.

"What followed surprised him. Miraculously clearing the stabilzer, he tumbled into a new world. The noise inside the cockpit had been deafening, as though one were rolling down a steep hill in an iron barrel, on fire, with a lot of people throwing rocks. A split second later everything became peaceful and quiet, churchlike. The silence was reassuring and revealing. From below he could hear an airplane running up its engines on an airfield near Tunis. He also heard a bell ringing somewhere, and a dog barking. It all seemed unreal.

"But reality soon reasserted itself. Earlier Cy had discovered he could feel the rudder controls better if he dispensed with the encumbering footwear. So that day, as usual, he had left his shoes off and was wearing only his loose-fitting winter flying boots. Just after he pulled the rip cord, the shock from the opeing parachute forced his boots off. Feeling the tug on his feet, Cy instinctively glanced downward. It was then that he saw the water. The thought of his careful preparations conforted him greatly. But another source of anxiety appeared immediately as Cy looked back up to see his assailant's Me-109 closing in. Fearing the worst, he was astonished to see the aircraft enter a circular pattern around him. The German pilot grinned and saluted as he passed by.

"Cy quickly turned his attention back to the dreaded water landing. He had rehearsed it well in his mind and knew exactly what to do. In a crouch with feet held together in case there was floating debris, Cy splashed down. For the third time in the space of a few minutes he was surprised. He had landed in one foot of water and two feet of mud.

"With the Mediterranean at his back and Germans coming toward him with weapons drawn, he attempted to sink his maps and other escape aids. But the items refused to sink in the shallow water and remained in clear view. Cy raised his hands and proceeded slowly toward his captors."

"Bub Clark also found himself somewhat surprised by the sequence of events after his capture in July 1942. After being checked in by a POW processing officer who took his name, rank, and serial number, Clark was taken to an officer's quarters to await the Luftwaffe. He was given a Sunday-night supper and then driven by a senior Luftwaffe officer and two guards to the Luftwaffe Officers' Club in Saint-Omer, one of the main bases of Fighter Command West. There he was interviewed by fighter pilots who had been involved in the afternoon fight and by an intelligence officer. Their primary interest, he concluded, was to discover who shot him down, as each one wanted credit. From Saint-Omer Clark was taken to the army military jail in Boulogne for the night. Early the next morning he was put on a train, the Dunord, and escorted to Brussels by one NCO and two privates. From there he took an evening train to Germany and, after two nights' traveling, arrived at Frankfurt. In a few hours he would be in Dulag Luft, the main Luftwaffe interrogation center, tired and harried, but certainly not abused.

"As Cy approached the Germans he extended his gun to them, butt first. He had walked only a few feet when a photographer drew near and a jeep suddenly appeared with a pilot dressed in desert flying gear. The pilot was introduced to him as Sergeant Hafner, the man who shot him down. Hafner offered Cy a cigarette. Not a smoker but still dazed, Cy took the cigarette and lit it. Then, noticing that Cy was an officer, Sergeant Hafner saluted him. A friendly discussion ensued, a mixture of pleasantries and questions about where Cy was born. Cy considered himself a 'name, rank, and serial number' man and refused to give away information he thought might be used against him later. He named the city of Philadelphia, a place he had never even visited. During the conversation the photographer took pictures at a furious rate. When Cy commented on the helmet a German was wearing, they asked him if he wanted to try it on. He said he would; he put it on and smiled. The photographer quickly captured the scene.

"Cy was impressed by the man who had shot him down. Seeing something hanging around the sergeant's neck, he hesitantly asked if it was a Ritter Croix (Knight's Cross). Hafner said it was. Upon closer inspection, Cy noticed the Eichenlaub (oak leaf) cluster as well. The sergeant was a highly decorated veteran. When he pointed out he was aware that Hafner must already have a distinguished military record, Hafner replied, 'Yes, you're the eighty-second airplane I've shot down.' Although not liking the outcome, Cy was somewhat relieved to learn that he had been outgunned by a true ace.

"After Cy commented on some of Hafner's other decorations, Hafner made a complimentary remark about Cy's set of wings. Cy immediately removed them from his uniform and said, 'Here, you can have them if you like. I don't think I'll need them where I'm going.' Then in a gesture of magnanimity, Hafner reached for his wings, saying 'Here, you can have mine too.' At that point, however, an officer stepped forward and said, 'No, you can't give this man anything—he's your prisoner.' Undaunted, Cy asserted, 'You tried to extend a friendly hand to me and I to you—if we both survive this war and our nations are back at peace again, come to the States sometime and visit me.' Then everyone present, including Cy, walked over to examine the ruins of his airplane.

"Upon leaving the scene, Cy was escorted to a house on rue de Plus in Tunis and incarcerated on the second floor. The windows were barred, and the guards appeared to be Hitler Youth or very young airmen, who were distinctly inclined to act like toughs. Cy wished his guards were more experienced soldiers, people who had been around long enough to recognize man's inhumanity to man and who, he believed, were likely to be more lenient. Somewhere along the way he ran into just such a person, a man who had worked as a butcher in Milwaukee and knew the area where Cy's two brothers lived on Fond du Lac Avenue. Cy appreciated the extra pieces of bread the man gave him from time to time and never forgot him.

"In addition to his concern about the guards, Cy knew that food, or rather the lack of it, was going to be a problem. Supper that first night consisted of one slice of German black bread and a little piece of sausage. In keeping with one of the names on his airplane, his gut began to growl and never stopped. Shortly thereafter, on the train to Rome, the transition from K-rations to German black bread and sauerkraut began to have its predictable effect. The ride north in the crowded cars was miserable for both him and the guards.

"Before continuing their journey, several thoughtful and trusting guards let Cy visit some of the sights in the Vatican. Once back on the train he traveled up the Po Valley and through the Brenner Pass. His impressions of captivity thus far were largely formed by the memorable exchange with the impressive young sergeant who shot him down."

"Spivey's trip [to Dulag Luft] only a few months later presaged the journeys others would experience. The war had raged for some time now, and more than a few nerves were beginning to fray.

"With pitchfork and rifle, the old man who captured Colonel Spivey marched him down the road toward home, which was about a mile from the crash. They entered his kitchen, and there was much loud talking and gesticulating between him and his wife, none of which Spivey understood. But he was pleased when they seated him and the woman brought him weak coffee, rich milk, and good bread. A half-hearted attempt to give him eggs wa abandoned when he declined the offer.

"By this time a distinctly friendly attitude seemed to prevail in the kitchen. Suddenly Spivey recalled that the briefing officer had told them that the Dutch and the French were friendly and might put them on the underground road to Spain. He got up, having rinsed his mouth with the coffee, and removed his helmet, and placed it on top of the cookstove. Then he spotted an old coat hanging on the wall. With much talk and waving of hands, he made it clear he wanted to put on the coat and get on with whatever was to come next. To his horror, the old woman let out a shriek as he moved toward the coat. In the same instant the farmer reappeared through the door, gun in hand and wearing a natty Landwehr uniform. He barked out a command in German. Spivey quickly realized that he was indeed their prisoner and made one desperate break for the door. Just as quickly the old man and his son barred the way.

"They took Spivey to the local constabulary of a nearby village. Soon he was joined by the rest of his crew, all except the gunner who had bailed out earlier than the rest to get medical aid. An attempt was made to load them on a Model T Ford bus to drive them to another village. But after a mile or so, the bus quit running, and everyone marched the rest of the day. As they walked, Spivey admired the way the Germans had managed to plant every square foot of soil along the way and kept their fields extremely neat.

"After a cold night of interrupted sleep, the Germans woke them about four o'clock in the morning, conducted a second search, and put them on another bus. This time the destintion was a Luftwaffe station near the town of Rheine. There they were given a drink of water, some sausage, and black bread and were put in solitary confinement in the post guardhouse. It was Spivey's first chance to think. Reflecting on the events of the past thirty-six hours, he thanked God that they were all safe from serious injury and death. Then he thought of his wife and son and found his throat closing tightly. He buried his face in his old winter flying cap and fell asleep.

"When Spivey complained of not feeling well, the Germans sent him to see the surgeon. His mouth and head hurt from the blow received in the crash, and his bowels had not functioned for three days. He asked for a laxative, but the Germans did not understand him—nor did he understand them. Efforts to communicate in French also failed, so he used sign language to tell them what was wrong. The Germans thought his bathroom antics hilarious and finally exclaimed, 'Ja, ja, ja!' In no time they produced a glass of milky liquid, and Spivey drank it. Then he realized they had mis- understood and had given him bismuth and charcoal to check the diarrhea that they thought he had. He was truly in trouble now. He

He went through the whole pantomime again, this time even getting so red in the face that blood vessels stood out on his neck and forehead. The Germans at last caught on and nearly burst with laughter. Spivey, however, looked at the box of pills they gave him. He clearly could see the word *cathartic*. As he was dismissed from the hospital he overheard someone remark, 'The colonel is not sick; he is crazy.'

"The fourth day they were given two days' rations and put on the train to Frankfurt. Spivey was surprised that the commuters paid them no attention at all, especially since they were closely guarded and readily recognizable in their aviators' togs. All ten of them were put into two compartments of a third-class train. As they proceeded he gazed into the damage inflicted upon hundreds of factories along the railway and wondered how long the Germans could take such a beating before they quit. At the same time he was amazed to see how quickly they had cleaned up the debris and how well the people were dressed.

"About midnight they came to East Cologne. There the fliers were taken off the train and led along dark, bomb-torn streets filled with soldiers. They crossed a huge bridge over the Rhine and suddenly realized they were standing beside the famous cathedral. The group paused for a moment to look. Suddenly four drunken German officers appeared and began to rant in German in a manner that made the Americans both angry and fearful. They picked on Spivey, presumably he unmistakably was the oldest and a colonel. When they got no response, one of them resorted to English. Breath laced with alcohol, he stuck his face close to Spivey's and told him what they were going to do to Luftgangsters who bombed their women and children and magnificent churches. Spivey could see that the cathedral had been hit several times and that not much remained of this once beautiful city. Lieutenant Wells started to answer back, but Spivey thought it best to remain quiet. The guards seemed to want to walk a fine line, cheerfully telling all enquirers who the Americans were and interceding only when they were about to be manhandled. In due time the guards moved the group along—to everyone's relief.

"Spivey had never dreamed that such total destruction was possible. Every building they saw from the Rhine to the far western side of the city was ruined. And once they got lost in the rubble.

One guard rousted some men who were sleeping in a basement and asked the way. By this time the Americans were so bewildered and frightened, it would not have surprised any of them if the Germans had shot them on the spot. The provocation, Spivey thought, must have been great enough for the inhabitants to commit such an act. Even there, where walls on either side stood more than four or five stories high, the first light of dawn was clearly discernible through the upper windows. It was a horrible sight. Yet in all his fear, confusion, and apathy, Spivey could not help feeling a fierce pride in the Allies' awakening military might. Audible expressions from the men confirmed his own feelings, and more than once he quieted them as they mumbled, 'This ought to teach the bastards!'

"The group reboarded the train in the busy station on the west side of the city, and Spivey was glad to leave the nightmarish world of Cologne. In contrast to the eerie atmosphere of that hellish, war-torn city at night, the daylight ride to Frankfurt was like traveling through a fairyland. The scenery was beautiful, and the war had not yet touched the area. Even under such difficult circumstances, Spivey appreciated the magnificence of the country-side.

"The luxuries, enjoyed primarily during the early years of the war, were of long-term benefit only to the few prisoners who served as part of the permanent staff at Dulag Luft. Most of the prisoners retained far more vivid memories of the unpleasant atmosphere in the interrogation center.

"After the guards who escorted the prisoners to the camp secured a receipt for their delivery, the captives were sent to the reception office. There, the staff's first task was to attempt to get the prisoners to reveal their identity, usually by ordering the officer prisoners to step forward and the 'other ranks' to line up behind them. 'to insure that they would not be separated and to allow them to go to the same camp.' If this ruse worked, and apparently it often did, the Germans had completed an important first step in the interrogation process. Knowledge of who belonged with whom on the various crews was a valuable tool in the interrogator's hands.

"One by one, the prisoners then filed into the Transport Office, where some personal information was noted and each man was thoroughly searched. All clothing down to their underwear was removed and methodically examined for weapons, escape aids, and personal property such as papers, pictures, and money.

"If the prisoner's comb. cigarettes, matches, money, etc., had not been taken earlier, the Germans now took such items, placed them in an envelope with his name on it, and gave assurances he would get them all back. Then each man was photographed and finger-printed. From the Transport Office, the airmen moved to one of three likely locations—the transit camp, the 'snake pit,' or a solitary confinement cell—depending upon the number of prisoners on hand at any one time. At the beginning of the war, virtually all prisoners went directly into the interrogation center. But their numbers increased from the dozen or so that arrived during the month of December 1939, to an average of 2,000 each month in 1944. When all available space in the interrogation center was in use, the camp staff sent prisoners to other places. Those thought to know little went to the transit camp after being briefly questioned. Prisoners who appeared to be a valuable source of information, but could not be immediately placed in solitary con-finement, usually went to the snake pit, a one-story building used as a way station. Spivey was sent there, and its nightmarish features were apparent right away, from the dirty rooms to the nasty guards. The small rooms contained an iron bed, a small table, a few chairs, and a slop jar. The single window was closed and locked, and the solid wood shutter, which opened and closed from the outside, was shut tight. The morning and evening meals usually consisted of one slice of heavy black bread with a thin coating of oleomargarine or ersatz jam, and a cup of lukewarm ersatz tea) made from various mixtures of hay, carrots, and parched grain) or ersatz coffee (composition unknown). For the noon meal, there was a good-sixed dish full of potato soup with large pieces of potatoes but no meat or fat. Spivey was not allowed to shave or brush his teeth, and only after much shouting and pleading did a guard let him out to use a filthy straddle latrine. Fortunately, the prisoners had to endure the snake pit for only a few days before being sent to the interrogation center.

"The center housed a confusing array of conditions and various forms of treatment. After 1941 the lmost prominent feature of this portion of the complex was the 'cooler.' This structure contained some two hundred forty solitary confinement cells into which each prisoner was thrust without ceremony. This was to be his home for an undetermined period of time during which he was cajoled, threatened, fed well, starved, treated to cigarettes and chocolate, or left to suffer nicotine fits and ponder his fate. All this was part of a sophisticated interrogation process that developed over months and years. During the early days of the war, attempts to obtain information in subtle ways were inefficient and feeble. Near the war's end, the operation was so effective and thorough-going that it produced for the Germans almost every bit of information they desired from the crews.

"Different explanations have been given for the center's success. Some say the prisoners talked because of fear or, conversely, because of German kindness. Others suggest that the captured airmen's security training had been inadequate, and so they were not prepared for the techniques used upon them during interrogation and either consciously or unconsciously gave away important military secrets. Hans Scharff, an interrogator at Dulag Luft, claims that the prisoners talked because the Germans' methods were 'almost irresistible.'

"Scharff's claim that the methods were almost irresistible is credible in the sense that the interrogation effort at Dulag Luft did not consist of a single act. The extended engagement was conducted by skillful men employing clever tactics of which the man being questioned often was totally unaware. A British report went so far as to credit the Germans with sometimes completely disguising the adversarial character of the interrogation. When this was achieved, the prisoner, after exhaustive and usually productive questioning, often wondered when the actual interrogation was going to begin.

"The interrogation process began innocuously when a man pretending to be a Red Cross representative entered the prisoner's cell and asked him to fill out a lengthy form. After the Allies protested such false practices, the interrogator no longer mentioned the Red Cross, but the illegal form continued to be used, apparently until the end of the war. According to the Geneva Convention, prisoners of war were obliged to give only their name, rank, and serial number. The German forms asked for this information first, but gradually verged into other areas. Most prisoners gave the required data, paused a little on the questions about their home address, the names of next of kin, and civilian employment, and stopped writing altogether when they came to questions about the number and location of their flying units and other military information.

"The Germans made maximum use of this preliminary session. In addition to the information obtained on the 'Red Cross' form, they had an opportunity to evaluate the prsioner's character. After leaving the cell, the men conducting the session often wrote telling statements that helped in later interrogations, describing the prisoner as a 'heavy smoker' or noting that he was 'unsure of himself and susceptible to flattery.' Furthermore, when the prisoner announced he could not supply the requested information, the interrogator usually displayed a pained look. How else could they prove the prisoner's claims that he was in fact a flier and not a spy or a saboteur? Surely the airman was telling the truth, but (in a lowered voice) the Gestapo was not so easily convinced. Some of the ways in which the Gestapo secured information did not bear thinking about, especially since the interrogator too was a military man, a man of honor, and understood such things in a way the security police did not. The object of this entire exchange, of course, was to impress upon the prisoner the importance of giving sufficient information to establish his identity beyond any doubt. The interrogator argued that at the minimum, the prisoner had to reveal his flying unit. Then, alone in his cell, he contemplated the last words about the Gestapo.

"The small cell was ten and one-half feet long, five and one-half feet wide, and had an eight-foot ceiling. The airman sat alone with his thoughts. There was nothing to divert his attention. The furnishings consisted usually of a bed, one stool, and two blankets. No reading or writing materials were available, and the one light was turned on and off at random from somewhere outside the cell. Outside switches also controlled the temperature of the heaters, a source of much suffering for the prisoners. Frequently the temperature in the room became almost unbearable, rising high enough at times to singe a towel laid on the radiator and making the bed and all metal hot enough to scorch bare flesh. The thick cement walls retained the heat like a sauna, and the one window in the room was painted over. The Germans insisted that the construction of the walls prevented communication between the prisoners and that the occasional high temperatures resulted from breakdowns in the heating system, explanations considered inadequate both during and after the war. The effect on the prisoners was predictable. When the time came for them to be taken from their cells for interrogation, they were relieved and thankful just to be momentarily out of confinement. This feeling of gratitude played an important role during the second session."

"The first interrogator had by this time turned over all his data to another, one carefully chosen to deal with the particular prisoner. The man who now conducted the interrogation was a specialist who handled only crewmen from bombers, or fighters, or whatever his area of expertise might be. All the interrogators spoke excellent English and had lived for extended periods of time in Allied countries. Most of them were good judges of character and had a large array of techniques to employ against the captives.

"Taking advantage of the prisoner's sense of relief at being let out of solitary confinement, the interrogator usually began in a friendly manner, offering cigarettes or chocolate and engaging in light conversation about war's unfortunate effects, sports, music and art, some aspect of life in the captive's native country, or the mutual problems of military men. Skillfully the interrogator sought to make the prisoner feel safe and relaxed.

"These circumstances made it difficult for the prisoner to stick to name, rank, and serial number. Officers found it particularly hard to remain silent, for the majority felt that their breeding and background required them to duel verbally with their interrogator on such obviously innocent matters. Unfortunately, every word they spoke to relieve their sense of being ill at ease gave the interrogator a handle. Not unexpectedly, the enlisted prisoners did not respond in the same way. As one report noted, the sergeants mostly 'felt no compunction about being stubborn to the point of downright rudeness; they were less easily flattered than officers, and they had fewer delusions about the real purpose of the interrogator's conversation. The average sergeant felt instinctively that he was not sufficiently important to warrant as much attention out of pure chivalry, and to this extent officers as a class were easier to interrogate than were the enlisted men.

"If the prisoner was able to withhold the desired information throughout extended friendly conversations, threats of violence abruptly followed. The primary threat, that the captor would be turned over to the Gestapo, was employed most effectively when the prisoner refused to identify his unit. The interrogator repeatedly insisted that this information was needed to prove the subject's claim that he was an aviator. Until such proof was given, he reminded the prisoner, no word would be sent out regarding his capture. This thought naturally caused considerable anxiety, since the men knew their loved ones back home had received word they were missing in action, but not that they were alive and well in a German prison camp. Furthermore, they knew that until the Red Cross received information about their captivity, the Germans could kill or otherwise keep them hidden away for years, all the while claiming they had never been captured. Jews were told they might be subjected to persecution, and whenever the Germans learned a prisoner had relatives in German-held territory, they suggested what might happen if he did not talk. Usually the session served to create a great deal of uncertainty in the prisoners' minds.

"Except in rare cases, the threats were not carried out. Nor was physical violence relied upon—the possible exception was an occasional slap on the face. The interrogators prided themselves on being able to get the information they wanted without resorting to such vulgar tactics. And the results seemed to bear out their claim.

"The Germans also used subtle but effective bribery to capitalize upon the prisoner's awareness of his physical discomfort. The offer of a cigarette, a drink, a parole walk or trip to the camp cinema, a promise to expedite notifying the prisoner's next of kin that he was safe, or a pledge that members of a crew would be allowed to remain together, all served to throw the prisoner off stride. The Germans knew better than to ask for something directly in return. They were satisfied that prisoners accepting such favors would likely feel a little indebted to them in a more friendly and trusting way than before. An interrogator would turn this asset to his own use at a later time.

"Sometimes the interrogator totally disarmed the prisoner by demonstrating how much the Germans knew—so he no longer needed to remain silent. Much to the prisoner's dismay, the interrogator usually possessed an amazing arsenal of facts. It was demoralizing that the Germans could often cite the prisoner's unit number, the location of the unit, the name of its commander or other notable personnel, the types of aircraft it possessed, the missions it had undertaken, possibly some of the missions planned for it, and a seemingly infinite list of other details that left the prisoner astonished and convinced that the Germans did in fact know everything they wanted to know.

"Colonel Spivey was indeed surprised by what the interrogator knew about him. Saying that Spivey really did not have to worry about giving away any secrets because the Germans already knew all about him anyway, the interrogator produced a picture of the flying personnel of an 8th Air Force group and the group commander and his staff. He told Spivey about the group he had flown with and the names of the crew members, that he had a wife and a child whose birthday would come two days later, where he had been throughout his service, and wound up by saying Spivey should have had his big feet on his desk at Maxwell Field, Alabama, instead of trying to find out why so many Allied bombers were being shot down over Germany. The information shocked Spivey. He was in Europe on secret orders and was certain that not a person on the crew knew about his job or mission, much less anything about his wife or his child's birth date. Somewhat awed, he filled out the 'Red Cross' form, leaving out the data concerning his group. The interrogator obligingly filled it in for him. As a parting shot he told Spivey he was lucky his previously scheduled mission to the ball-bearing works at Schweinfurt had been scrubbed twice, because the Luftwaffe had been waiting and would be again whenever the attack took place. Spivey had in fact been posted to go on one of the flights. And the next day his spirits plummeted when he heard the anti-aircraft guns and saw American bombers being viciously attacked by German fighters as they engaged in the shuttle raid from England to North Africa that was a diversion for the long-awaited Schweinfurt raid.

"What happened to the prisoners at Dulag Luft constituted yet one more ingredient in the bond of experience shared by the men sent to Stalag Luft III. Most of them did not leave Dulag Luft burdened with a sense of guilt, sincerely believing they had not given any important informtion to the Germans. The did, however, leave with a heightened respect for German thoroughness, organization, and intelligence-gathering ability.

"After a stay of one or two weeks (but sometimes as long as a month or more), the prisoners were sent to a transit camp and then on to a permanent camp, usually in groups or 'purges' of fifty to one hundred men. The three-hundred-mile trip from Dulag Luft to Sagan usually proved to be yet another ordeal. Frequently the men were packed into the forty-and-eight boxcars taken from the French. The cars had often been used to haul livestock, and it was not unusual to find fresh manure or an inch of black dirt on the floor. Sometimes the Germans ordered several prisoners to clean out the cars. There were a few boards for the prisoners to lie down on, and the arrangement depended on the number of people. Since the cars were almost always filled beyond capacity, the majority had to remain standing or sit on the filty floor.

"The prisoners suffered other discomforts on the trip as well. Although there usually was enough food, drinking water often was withheld for periods of twenty-four hours or longer. There were no toilet facilities, and the men were unable to relieve themselves except perhaps in a nearby woods or a marshaling yard when the train stopped. Little effort was made to provide any privacy for the prisoners, and often there were women in the vicinity.

"The cars were poorly ventilated and the inside became oppressive as the train proceeded on its jerky way. Since this transport was assigned a low priority, the prison cars were hitched to the end of one freight train after another and shunted on and off railroad sidings. The trip took two days or longer, and often exposed the prisoners to bombing and strafing attacks by Allied aircraft.

"When the train finally arrived at the station in Sagan, the tired and dirty travelers got out and walked the short distance to the camp. While at the transit camp, many had heard detailed accounts of the country-club atmosphere at Stalag Luft III, which reportedly contained swimming pools and golf courses. Few prisoners entertained any delusions about what lay ahead, and they certainly did not believe such stories, but they did look forward to seeing their new home so they could size it up for themselves. They also welcomed being able to establish some kind of routine after the hectic uncertainty of recent days. And they knew that old friends would be there, many of whom they had thought were dead but whose they had seen on the register at the transit camp. With a swirl of such thoughts running through their minds, the prisoners stepped beyond the edge of the forest separating the railway station from the camp and gazed for the first time upon the maze of barbed wire and gray buildings of Stalag Luft III.

"Tension was high when Bub Clark walked into East Compound of Stalag Luft III in August 1942. It was not a good day for a new prisoner to arrive. Everybody's nerves were on edge. There had been a direct confrontation between the prisoners and a large contingent of heavily armed guards earlier in that morning. The focus of attention had been Douglas Bader, the famed legless fighter pilot who antagonized the Germans from the moment he was shot down. Having earlier lost his legs in an airplane crash, he had tin ones made. Then he had defied the odds and learned all over again to fly. When his plane was hit and he discovered the tin legs were caught, he simply unstrapped them and bailed out. He both intrigued and angered his captors. Having allowed an English aircraft safe passage to drop him another pair of legs, they were rewarded with Bader's continuous escape efforts and the most antagonistic personality many of them had ever encountered. Once in Stalag Luft III, Bader riled the prisoners so much that the Germans decided they had to move him to Colditz, a prison reserved for the most avid, troublesome escapers. Bader threatened to jump in the fire pool so the Germans would have to swim in after him, an act calculated to embarrass and humiliate them. The Senior British Officer talked him out of it, but Bader received satisfaction anyway. Feeling that his forced removal might cause a riot, the Germans took the precaution of sending armed guards to lead him out. Bader sneered with glee as he left, knowing the other prisoners would not miss the significance of two columns of armed Germans escorting one solitary man who had no legs. So the prisoners had their day, but lost the battle of keeping Bader with them. Consequently, their mood was almost as foul as the Germans'. Bub was led into the camp and shown to his bunk. Still almost warm, it was Bader's.

"The long-awaited South Compound opened [at Stalag Luft III] on September 8, 1943. Virtually all American prisoners previously detained in North Compound, plus a number of Americans from

Center Compound and from the now German controlled prisoner of war camps in Italy, moved into South. Thus from the beginning, South was occupied by experienced individuals capable of organizing themselves and operating in accordance with proven methods. The guiding spirit in the community-building effort in South Compound was Colonel [Charles] Goodrich, commanding officer of the prisoners assigned to South from the time the compound opened until the end of the war.

"South compound was considerably smaller than North, but it contained the same number of buildings—sixteen. The sports field was about one-third as large as the one found in North. In the beginning there were stumps all over the compound, and the prisoners removed them over a period of months. The work started in the area set aside for the athletic field. The buildings were constructed of prefabricated materials made of wood, and the fourteen barracks were self-contained. Each one had an indoor latrine with one urinal and two commodes, a washroom with six porcelain washbasins, and a kitchen with one cookstove. The indoor latrine was for use at night, and the pit-latrines were utilized during the day. The rooms varied in size and accommodated from two to ten people, the largest room measuring sixteen by twenty-eight feet. Each barracks could comfortably house 72 officers and 12 enlisted men, or a total of 84 people. The entire compound could thus hold about 1,175 men without overcrowding. The Germans placed a shower hut in the compound, but for more than nine months failed to provide the equipment necessary for its operation. So the prisoners had no hot showers and had to settle for hose-and-punched can devices. The compound also contained a large cook-house and a theater built by the prisoners.

"The heavy influx of prisoners throughout the summer and fall of 1943—the result of increased bombing activity—soon filled the barracks in every compound to capacity. In October the British began to put eight men in the six-man rooms. In November the same process was initiated in South Compound. Fortunately, crowding had not yet become a problem.

At age sixty-one, Colonel Friedrich-Wilhelm von Lindeiner-Wildau was tormented by divided loyalties when he took over as comm-

marrow of his bones, von Lindeiner clearly had not shown the same affection for the new Nazi regime. He wanted to retire and simply fade from the scene, but the authorities would not let him go. As a professional soldier, he never gave a thought to insubordination. Somehow he would have to fulfill his assigned duties in this twilight world where the high ideals and values of the past were being subjugated to political and military expediencies, the full consquences of which few could yet guess. His independent actions would get him into trouble sooner or later, of that he was almost certain. The more important question for him, however, was whether he could remain true to his principles when such things no longer seemed to matter. He was proud to serve his beloved Germany, but he dreaded the thought of waking up someday, no longer knowing who he was or what he stood for.

"When the German and prisoner administrative systems worked in tandem the prisoners obtained the essentials of life, though not without some difficulty. The captives and their captors, however, still represented opposing sides in a bitter war, and it would have been too much to expect continued cooperation in everything affecting the vital interests of either the prisoners or the Germans. The Germans often ignore the prisoners' urgent needs in order to devote more of their resources to the war. At times they also fell victim to their own propaganda about the terrible and visious Luftgangsters: prisoners' relatively minor infractions prompted reprisals of unwarranted severity. At the same time, the prisoners never tired in their efforts to escape and to 'keep the Germans busy.' They understood the possible penalties if they were caught in their forbidden acts and were willing to accept the consequences as long as they were not too severe. But they would not accept unnecessary privations and looked to their organizational structure and sense of identity as a community to help fill the voids or overcome any unreasonableness in the German administrative system. In the final analysis, they fully grasped the importance of helping themselves and proceeded to do so on a routine basis in order to achieve the best possible living conditions and the most meaningful approach to life that circumstances permitted."

Bibliography

Andrews, Allen, *Exemplary Justice*, London, 1976

Barker, A.J., *Prisoners of War*, New York, 1975

Bennett, John M, *Memoirs*, ca 1950

Brickhill, Paul, *The Great Escape*, Greenwich, Conn., 1950

Crawley, Aidan, *Escape from Germany*, New York, 1956

Dennett, Carl, *American Prisoners of War*, 1918

Dominy, John, *The Sergeant Escapers*, London, 1974

Freeman, Roger, *The Hub*, Shrewsbury, England, 1988

Geneva Convention Relative to the Treatment of Prisoners of War, Geneva, 1960

Haugland, Vern, *The Eagle Squadrons*, New York, 1979

Kaplan, Philip and Smith, Rex, *One Last Look*, New York, 1983

Lavender, E. & Sheffe, N., *The Evaders*, Toronto, 1992

von Lindeiner-Wildau, *Memoirs*, Durand, A and Geiss, B

Mahurin, Walker, *Hitler's Fall Guys*, Atglen, PA., 1999

Philpot, Oliver, *Stolen Journey*, New York, 1952

Simmons, Kenneth, *Kriegie*, New York, 1960

Toliver, Raymond, *The Interrogator*, Fallbrook, CA., 1978

Vietor, John, *Time Out*, New York, 1951

Williams, Eric, *The Wooden Horse*, New York, 1949

Yeager, Chuck and Janos, Leo, *Yeager*, New York, 1985

Zemke, Hubert and Freeman, Roger, *Zemke's Stalag*, Shrewsbury, England, 1991